1000 Harry Po

Mera Wolfe

Introduction

1000 Harry Potter Facts is packed with all the trivia you could ever wish to know about this beloved series of fantasy books and films!

(1) Nicolas Flamel was a real person. He was a French scribe and manuscript-seller. After his death, Flamel developed a reputation as an alchemist believed to have discovered the philosopher's stone and to have thereby achieved immortality. These legendary accounts first appeared in the 17th century.

(2) JK Rowling says that Hermione was very important in the books because she used this character to deliver exposition. "If you need to tell your readers something just put it in her. There are only two characters that you can put it convincingly into their dialogue. One is Hermione, the other is Dumbledore. In both cases you accept, it's plausible that they have, well Dumbledore knows pretty much everything anyway, but that Hermione has read it somewhere. So, she's handy."

(3) Butterbeer in Harry Potter is a drink made with butterscotch. It is most likely based on a real beverage called Buttered Beer which was drunk in Tudor times. Buttered beer was made with beer, eggs, sugar, nutmegs and cloves.

(4) Until Marvel's Avengers franchise and a fresh slate of Star Wars films came along, Harry Potter was briefly the most successful film franchise of all time and edged out another famous British hero - James Bond 007 - to claim this mark. According to Box Office Mojo, the first six adaptations of JK Rowling's books earned an astonishing $5.4 billion worldwide - not adjusted for inflation. This took it past the Bond series. As far as longevity goes though, the James Bond franchise is still the most enduringly indestructible franchise. The first Bond film was made way back in 1962.

(5) Legend has it that Michael Gambon fell asleep while shooting Dumbledore's death scene!

(6) JK Rowling says that Shakespeare's Macbeth was an inspiration on the prophecy about Harry and Voldemort. "I

absolutely adore Macbeth. It is possibly my favourite Shakespeare play. And that's the question isn't it? If Macbeth hadn't met the witches, would he have killed Duncan? Would any of it have happened? Is it fated or did he make it happen? I believe he made it happen."

(7) In the Harry Potter film series, the thousands of props needed five large warehouses to store them. The props included 5000 pieces of furniture, 40000 Weasley's Wizard Wheezes and 25000 pages of the Quibbler.

(8) The Legend of King Arthur is an obvious influence on Harry Potter. "Gryffindor's sword owes something to the legend of Excalibur, the sword of King Arthur, which in some legends must be drawn from a stone by the rightful king," said JK Rowling. "The idea of fitness to carry the sword is echoed in the sword of Gryffindor's return to worthy members of its true owner's house."

(9) There are some unmistakable similarities between Harry Potter and The Worst Witch by Jill Murphy. The Worst Witch was a series of books first published in the early 1970s. The Worst Witch is set at a boarding-school for girls called Miss Cackle's Academy for Witches. The school is a castle surrounded by an enchanted forest. There is a teacher of potions and Miss Cackle's Academy was founded by a witch called Hermione! There have been some TV shows based on the Worst Witch books.

(10) The staircase at Hogwarts has 250 paintings in total.

(11) At a press conference for one of the early Harry Potter films, an American journalist asked a twelve year-old Rupert Grint how much the child actors were getting paid. Grint replied that he didn't understand muggle money. The producers thought this was a very clever answer!

(12) The Deathly Hallows was based on The Pardoner's Tale by Geoffrey Chaucer.

(13) The Black Sisters in Harry Potter were probably inspired by the real life Mitford Sisters Unity and Diana. The Mitfords were from an aristocratic English family of socialites and became notorious for their support of fascism. Unity Mitford worshipped Adolf Hitler while Diana Mitford married British fascist leader Oswald Mosley.

(14) Universal Orlando Resort's Wizarding World of Harry Potter sent people to England to sample traditional British pub food in order to create menus for their attraction. They even consulted JK Rowling to get some tips on what food would be authentic to serve in a Harry Potter theme park.

(15) Christmas pudding is mentioned in the Harry Potter books. This has its origins in medieval England and is sometimes known as plum pudding. This is a very rich dark pudding made with fruits and spices. It is still something of a tradition to eat this on Christmas Day in Britain. Christmas pudding is usually served with cream or (if you are more adventurous) set alight and served with brandy butter.

(16) JK Rowling says she regrets her decision to kill off Florean Fortescue.

(17) Harry Potter and the Deathly Hallows Part 2 was the biggest grossing film in the film series with over one billion dollars in worldwide receipts.

(18) The 1985 adventure film Young Sherlock Holmes is a big influence on the Harry Potter film series. Young Sherlock Holmes depicts a young Holmes (Nicholas Rowe) and Watson (Alan Cox) meeting at the exclusive Brompton Academy as schoolboys and shows us how they become friends and solve their first mystery together. One can see the influences on

Potter with the young cast and anachronistic boarding school setting. It comes as no surprise that when the casting was under way for the first Potter film, prospective actors were asked to perform scenes from Young Sherlock Holmes. Chris Columbus, who wrote Young Sherlock Holmes, directed the first Harry Potter film. "That was sort of a predecessor to this movie, in a sense", he told the BBC in 2001, "It was about two young boys and a girl in a British boarding school who had to fight a supernatural force."

(19) American child actor Liam Aiken was the initial choice of Chris Columbus to play Harry Potter in the first film. However, JK Rowling insisted that the parts had to be played by British actors so that all the accents would be authentic. This meant some big Hollywood stars had their hopes of being in the film dashed. Robin Williams was very keen to play Hagrid but JK Rowling already had her heart set on Robbie Coltrane for this part.

(20) JK Rowling suffered from writer's block when working on Chamber of Secrets. "That was the only book in which I've had writer's block. In fact I doubt whether it was true writer's block. I think it was panic because I got this big burst of publicity for Philosopher's Stone and I froze. I thought Chamber of Secrets would never be as good. I think it was panic rather than actual lack of ideas. The publicity happened when the American deal happened. Before that, sales of Philosopher's Stone had been climbing very healthily for a completely unknown book so people were getting interested, but only in the book trade. Then Arthur Levine in America bought Philosopher's Stone for the American market for what I think may have been an unprecedented amount of money for a completely unknown children's book. And then people sat up and looked around and thought 'Well, what happened there? Why is that worth all that money?' and then I had a lot of press interest - it seemed like a lot to me at the time. Looking back, it probably wasn't that much."

(21) Daniel Radcliffe's parents were nervous about Daniel playing the part of Harry Potter. They were concerned about his schooling and how he would cope with immense fame at such a young age.

(22) Chris Columbus said that they specifically chose child actors from stable family backgrounds to mitigate the 'child star curse'. He said you had to audition the parents as much as you auditioned the children.

(23) Casting director Janet Hirshenson says there was a big push by the studio to cast Billy Elliot star Jamie Bell as Harry in the first film. However, at 14, Bell was ultimately considered a bit on the old side to play the young Harry at the start of his wizarding adventures.

(24) Leadenhall Market is used in Harry Potter and the Philosopher's Stone as the exterior for Diagon Alley and the Leaky Cauldron. Leadenhall Market is a beautiful covered market in the City of London.

(25) Mince pies are mentioned in the Harry Potter books. This is a very traditional sweet English pie. It is shortcrust pastry filled with dried fruits and spices called 'mincemeat' (though it contains neither meat nor mince). Mince pies are a big tradition in Britain at Christmas.

(26) JK Rowling was slightly surprised that the Harry Potter books were so popular with adults (in addition to the children they were primarily aimed at). "That was a bit of a shock to me because I'd been writing for adults before and the manuscripts were never publishable. Then, I write what I think is a child's story-although really I wrote it for me, primarily for me. In fact, when I first started writing, I think I was thinking too much about the children who would read it. So, I thought, okay, just write it for yourself. And that was the

right decision, because then, as a writer, you can't talk down to your audience. When fan letters started coming in to both publishers, in Britain and in the U.S., many were from adults who weren't even saying, 'My daughter read it,' but they were saying things like, 'I bought it, I read it, I love it. Can I join the fan club?' And those comments were from a woman who was 60 years old. That was amazing."

(27) Hagrid is fond of mead. Mead or honey wine is made by fermenting honey with water. Like beer, mead is sometimes flavoured with fruits, spices, grains or hops.

(28) In 2020, it was reported that a newly discovered species of snake in India was given the name Salazar Slytherin.

(29) Scholastic wanted to call the first book 'Harry Potter and the School of Magic' in the United States but JK Rowling thought this was a terrible title.

(30) The many books in Dumbledore's office were conveyed in an ingenious and cost effective way by the props department for the film series. They simply bound hundreds of old telephone directories in leather.

(31) The divination textbook at Hogwarts was by Cassandra Vablatsky. This name is inspired by Helena Blavatsky - a late 19th century mystic, occultist, and medium.

(32) In 2020, it was reported that three rare editions of Harry Potter books were saved from a landfill site in Buckinghamshire. A school was clearing out its library but - luckily - a teacher managed to save the books from a skip. The books were a first edition hardback of Harry Potter and The Philosopher's Stone and two paperback first editions of the same novel. There are not many copies of these early editions still floating around so the books were worth thousands of pounds.

(33) Philosopher's stone, in Western alchemy, means an unknown substance, also called the tincture or the powder, sought by alchemists for its supposed ability to transform base metals into precious ones, especially gold and silver. Alchemists also believed that an elixir of life could be derived from it.

(34) The 'Seven Potters' scene in the film series required at least ninety takes to get right because it was so complicated.

(35) Harry simply HAD to be an orphan according to JK Rowling. "Of course it's been done before, but Harry HAD to be an orphan - so that he's a free agent, with no fear of letting down his parents, disappointing them, and Hogwarts HAS to be a boarding school - half the important stuff happens at night! Then there's the security. Having a child of my own reinforces my belief that children above all want security, and that's what Hogwarts offers Harry."

(36) The breakfast tables at Hogwarts contain bacon, butter, corn flakes, coffee, eggs, fried sausages, fried tomatoes, kippers, marmalade and jam, milk, orange juice, porridge in tureens, pumpkin juice, rolls salt, tea, toast.

(37) The 1986 comedy fantasy film Troll has a character named Harry Potter and themes of magic. Coincidence? John Buechler, the director of the film, claims that JK Rowling was influenced by the film. For her part, Rowling says the name Harry Potter came from a childhood friend named Ian Potter and Harry being her favourite male Christian name.

(38) Harry Potter is a big fan of treacle tart. Treacle tart is a British dessert that was first mentioned by Mary Jewry in her cookbooks from the late 19th century. Treacle tart is made with shortcrust pastry and golden syrup.

(39) Over three thousand girls turned up at the film auditions to find Cho Chang.

(40) Where did the idea of the Sorting Hat come from? "That was a bit of hard work," says JK Rowling. "First, I considered the many different ways we sort things. Pulling names out of a hat was the one that kept coming back to me. So I twisted the idea around and came up with a talking hat that could make decisions."

(41) Why did JK Rowling make her central hero a boy rather than a girl? "I don't know why that - why Harry came to me. No, I don't know why it was a boy. But have I given thought to it? Yes, definitely. I'd been writing the book for 6 months, and I did suddenly stop, and, I mean - it took me 6 months because I was enjoying myself so much - to suddenly stop myself and think 'hang on, I'm obviously female, and my hero is a boy! How did that happen?' But it was too late. It was too late, then, to make Harry Harriet. He was very real to me as a boy. I would have - you know, to put him in a dress would have felt like Harry in drag. I couldn't - I was too fond of him by then to go and turn him into a girl.

(42) JK Rowling says she came up with the name Inferi because she didn't want to use the term Zombie.

(43) JK Rowling feels that Phoenix was a little on the long side. "There are bits of all six books that I would go back and tighten up. My feeling is that Phoenix is overlong, but I challenge anyone to find the obvious place to cut. There are places that I would prune, now, looking back, but they wouldn't add up to a hugely reduced book, because my feeling is you need what's in there. You need what's in there if I'm going to play fair for the reader in the resolution in book seven. One of the reasons Phoenix is so long is that I had to move Harry around a lot, physically. There were places he had to go he had never been before, and that took time — to

get him there, to get him away. That was the longest non-Hogwarts stretch in any of the books, and that's really what bumps up the length. I'm trying to think of specifics, it's hard."

(44) The quote on the tombstone of Harry's parents ('And the last enemy that shall be destroyed is death') is from 1 Corinthians.

(45) JK Rowling filled up five pages of a notebook before settling on the word Quidditch. "I love making up words. There are a few key words in the books that wizards know and muggles, as in us no-magic-people, don't know. Well, muggle is an obvious example. Then there's quidditch. Quidditch is the wizarding sport. A journalist in Britain asked me... She said to me, "now, you obviously got the word "quidditch" from "quiddity," meaning the essence of a thing, it's proper nature," and I was really really tempted to say, "yes, you're quite right," because it sounded so intellectual, but I had to tell her the truth, which was that I wanted a word that began with Q -- on a total whim -- and I filled about, I don't know, 5 pages of a notebook with different Q -words until I hit quidditch and I knew that was the perfect one - when I finally hit quidditch."

(46) Hermione is described in the books as a young girl with 'lots of bushy brown hair and rather large front teeth'. Emma Watson tried to wear false front teeth to play the character when she was cast as Hermione but it impaired her ability to deliver dialogue so this plan was abandoned.

(47) Michael Gambon, who replaced the late Richard Harris in the role of Professor Albus Dumbledore, has never read any of the Harry Potter books.

(48) Rupert Grint had never done any professional acting before he was cast as Ron.

(49) A man in America legally changed his name to Lucius Malfoy and then named his house Malfoy Manor!

(50) JK Rowling says Parselmouth is an old word for someone who has a problem with their mouth like a hair lip.

(51) Dumbledore is over a hundred years old. "I have said before that wizards unless they contract some horrible magical disease, which does happen, live a long time," said JK Rowling.

(52) The original name for the Death Eaters was Knights of Walpurgis.

(53) The Peppermint Toads on sale at the Harry Potter Studio Tour in London are often described as tasting like After Eight Mints.

(54) Voldemort made an appearance during the opening ceremony of the London 2012 Summer Olympics as a 100-foot inflatable Dark Lord.

(55) Harry Potter and the Philosopher's Stone is one of only a handful of books to have sold more than a hundred million copies. Others in this select club include The Lord of the Rings and Alice's Adventures in Wonderland.

(56) Hedwig's name was inspired by Saint Hedwig of Silesia. Hedwig was Duchess of Silesia from 1201 and of Greater Poland from 1231 as well as High Duchess consort of Poland from 1232 until 1238. She cared for the sick and orphans and used her money to found hospitals.

(57) It is estimated that Daniel Radcliffe got through around eighty prop wands during the course of the films.

(58) Daniel Radcliffe was supposed to wear green contact

lenses in the films but he found he was allergic to them.

(59) JK Rowling has described Wart from TH White's The Sword In The Stone as "Harry's spiritual ancestor".

(60) A galleon is worth about five pounds but it depends on the exchange rate.

(61) So many fans visit King's Cross station to take pictures of platforms 9 and 10 that the station management put up a sign that says Platform 9 ¾.

(62) King's Cross is important to JK Rowling because that's where her parents met.

(63) JK Rowling says she first came up for the idea for Harry Potter while on a train from Manchester to London in 1990. "In 1990, my then-boyfriend and I decided to get a flat and move to Manchester together. We would flat hunt every once in awhile. One weekend after flat hunting, I took the train back to London on my own, and the idea for Harry Potter fell into my head. I didn't have a pen and was too shy to ask anyone for one on the train, which frustrated me at the time, but when I look back it was the best thing for me. It gave me the full four hours on the train to think up all the ideas for the book."

(64) The third smell Hermione recognises in the Amortentia potion is that of Ron's hair.

(65) Robbie Coltrane's stunt and body-double as the half-giant Hagrid was the 6'10 former rugby player Martin Bayfield. Bayfield won 31 England caps and played three times for the British & Irish Lions.

(66) JK Rowling had this to say of Harry's scar - "I wanted him to be physically marked by what he has been through. It was an outward expression of what he has been through inside. I

gave him a scar and in a prominent place so other people would know him. It is almost like being the chosen one, or the cursed one, in a sense. Someone tried to kill him; that's how he got it. I chose the lightning bolt because it was the most plausible shape for a distinctive scar. As you know, the scar has certain powers, and it gives Harry warnings."

(67) The four houses at Hogwarts refer to the four elements. Gryffindor is fire, Ravenclaw is air, Hufflepuff is earth and Slytherin is water.

(68) Steven King called Dolores Umbridge the "greatest make-believe villain to come along since Hannibal Lecter."

(69) A dessert known as a knickerbocker glory is mentioned in the Harry Potter books. A knickerbocker glory is served in a tall glass and usually contains ice cream, whipped cream, fruit, and syrup.

(70) Voldemort is incapable of love because he was conceived under the effects of a love potion.

(71) Mattel released a Harry Potter Mystery at Hogwarts board game that was inspired by Cluedo. In the game you have to become a magical detective and work out who broke the instruction of Dumbledore by casting a magic spell and also determine where this spell was cast. There are nine rooms from Hogwarts School in the game. The Great Hall, History of Magic Class, The Library, Potions Class, Transfiguration, Defence Against the Dark Arts, Filch's Office, Flying Class and Herbology. Players begin on the Hogwarts Seal ground floor and the player with the birthday nearest to Harry begins the game. The game was relatively well received.

(72) Professor Trelawney's great grandmother's name was Cassandra. In Greek mythology, Cassandra was a cursed seer who no one believed.

(73) How many wizards are there? This is JK Rowling on the subject - "Let's say three thousand [in Britain], actually, thinking about it, and then think of all the magical creatures, some of which appear human. So then you've got things like hags, trolls, ogres and so on, so that's really bumping up your numbers. And then you've got the world of sad people like Filch and Figg who are kind of part of the world but are hangers on. That's going to bump you up a bit as well, so it's a more sizable, total magical community that needs hiding, concealing, but don't hold me to these figures, because that's not how I think."

(74) When the film version of Harry Potter and the Philosopher's Stone was being planned, Steven Spielberg looked set to direct at one point. Spielberg spent around six months developing the film but his idea to make it as an animated feature was not what the studio or JK Rowling wanted. He eventually left the project. "I just felt that I wasn't ready to make an all-kids movie and my kids thought I was crazy," said Spielberg. "And the books were by that time popular, so when I dropped out, I knew it was going to be a phenomenon. But, you know I don't make movies because they're gonna to be phenomenons. I make movies because they have to touch me in a way that really commits me to a year, two years, three years of work."

(75) There are 10 different species of dragons in Harry Potter's universe.

(76) Harry, Ron, and Hermione have all graced Chocolate Frog cards.

(77) Out of all the books, Harry Potter and the Philosopher's Stone sold the most copies.

(78) A game of Quidditch will only end once the Golden

Snitch has been caught, or at the mutual consent of both team Captains.

(79) The Harry Potter books made JK Rowling a billionaire.

(80) Henry Cavill was nearly cast as Cedric Diggory. Cavill went on to play Superman in the DC superhero movies. By a quirk of fate, Robert Pattinson, who ended up playing Diggory, went on to be cast as Batman!

(81) In 1750, the British Ministry of Magic set down official rules for the game of Quidditch.

(82) The lowest-grossing Harry Potter film still made $90 million more than the biggest-grossing Twilight movie.

(83) Harry Potter and the Order of the Phoenix is the longest of the books and contains over a quarter of a million words.

(84) Ron Weasley was originally going to swear in the books from time to time but JK Rowling's publisher asked her to remove this.

(85) Ariana Grande is a huge Harry Potter fan. Ariana says her favourite Harry Potter characters are Draco Malfoy and Luna Lovegood.

(86) Hufflepuff is JK Rowling's favourite House.

(87) The casting director on the first Harry Potter film said it was obvious that Emma Watson was going to become a big star. She had a lot of confidence and composure for someone so young.

(88) The first book in the series had a slight title change in America - where it was called Harry Potter and the Sorcerer's Stone rather than Harry Potter and the Philosopher's Stone.

Arthur A. Levine, who purchased the American publishing rights for Scholastic, was worried that children in America might be put off by a book with 'Philosopher' in the title and felt that 'Sorcerer' made it sound more appealing for children.

(89) JK Rowling later said that she regretted allowing the American publisher change the title of the first book. "They changed the first title, but with my consent. To be honest, I wish I hadn't agreed now, but it was my first book, and I was so grateful that anyone was publishing me I wanted to keep them happy ..."

(90) The Harry Potter logo (where the 'P' in Potter becomes a lightning flash at the bottom) is very familiar from the films but made its debut in the first North American edition of the original Potter book. The logo was created by David Saylor - Art Director at Scholastic.

(91) "I have to admit," said David Saylor, "that I was little intimidated when I first started thinking about an illustrator for Harry Potter and the Sorcerer's Stone (Philosopher's Stone in the UK). Not because it was famous at that point, but because I liked the book so much I wanted to make sure I did it justice. I thought about it quite a bit: I tend to let things mull for a while until my feelings come to the surface. I'm fairly good at visualizing what I'm looking for once I know how I feel about something. Then I start looking at art samples. I had seen Mary GrandPré's work and I'd kept some samples in my art files. I pulled out her work, and the editor, Arthur Levine, was there with me at the time. As soon as I looked at her work, I had an A-Ha! moment. I knew she was right for the book. One sample in particular was of boy in a striped shirt walking among some ornamental hedges. It had the perfect combination, for me, of the ordinary and extraordinary."

(92) JK Rowling says that Goblet of Fire was going to be called The Doomspell Tournament at one point.

(93) JK Rowling says she does her best to shrug off religious criticism of the Harry Potter books. "Well, mostly I laugh about it. I ignore it... and very occasionally I get annoyed, because they have missed the point so spectacularly. I think the Harry books are very moral, but some people just object to witchcraft being mentioned in a children's book. Unfortunately, that means we'll have to lose a lot of classic children's fiction."

(94) JK Rowling says that if she could pick her own wand core it would be "Phoenix feather and... let's see... possibly walnut. I love walnut wood."

(95) The full name of Gryffindor's ghost Nearly Headless Nick is Sir Nicholas de Mimsy-Porpington.

(96) Lavender Brown is an anagram for brand new lover.

(97) Professor McGonagall was once a talented Quidditch player herself.

(98) JK Rowling turned down an offer to play Lily Potter in The Sorcerer's Stone. "I'm not really not cut out to be an actress, even one who just has to stand there and wave."

(99) How did JK Rowling invent the motto Never tickle sleeping dragons? "You know the way that most school slogans are thing like persevere and nobility, charity and fidelity or something, it just amused me to give an entirely practical piece of advice for the Hogwarts school motto. Then a friend of mine who is a professor of classics - my Latin was not up to the job, I did not think it should be cod Latin, it is good enough for cod Latin spells, that is they used to be a mixture of Latin and other things. When it came to a proper Latin slogan for the school I wanted it to be right, I went to him and asked him to translate. I think he really enjoyed it, he

rang me up and said, "I think I found the exactly right word, 'Titillandus'", that was how that was dreamt up."

(100) In total, there have been over 250 animals used in the Harry Potter film series.

(101) In a game of Quidditch, only the Keeper can block quaffle shots thrown by the opposing team.

(102) A war took place in the wizarding world at the same time as the Muggle Second World War. The evil wizard Grindelwald was defeated by Dumbledore in 1945, the same year as the Nazis surrendered.

(103) JK Rowling believes that Harry Potter is a good role model. "I see Harry as someone who is struggling to do the right thing, who is not without faults, who acts impetuously as you would expect someone of his age to act, but who is ultimately a very loyal person, and a very very courageous person. So, in as much as he has qualities that I admire most I would say he is a good role model. That doesn't mean that he is saintly, but then frankly, who is? But I think you do see enough of Harry's inner life, the workings of his mind in the books to know that he is ultimately human, struggling to do the right thing, which I think is admirable..."

(104) The driver and conductor of the Knight Bus were named after JK Rowling's grandfathers.

(105) A number of publishers rejected Harry Potter and the Philosopher's Stone because they felt it was a bit too long for a children's book.

(106) Hagrid could derive from the word haggard, meaning unruly or untidy looking.

(107) The maximum speed for a Firebolt broomstick is 150

mph.

(108) Daniel Radcliffe says he doesn't like the film version of Half-Blood Prince because he doesn't think he was very good in it.

(109) A phoenix was Dumbledore's Patronus.

(110) The French director Jean-Pierre Jeunet declined an offer to direct Harry Potter and the Order of the Phoenix. Jeunet is said to have felt that he would not have enjoyed the creative freedom he was accustomed to by working on a big studio film like Harry Potter.

(111) JK Rowling says she has no experience of boarding school - despite creating Hogwarts. "Well, the truth is, I've never been inside one, of course. I was comprehensive educated. But it was essential for the plot that the children could be enclosed somewhere together overnight. This could not be a day school, because the adventure would fall down every second day if they went home and spoke to their parents, and then had to break back into school every week to wander around at night, so it had to be a boarding school. Which was also logical, because where would wizards educate their children? This is a place where there were going to be lots of noises, smells, flashing lights, and you would want to contain it somewhere fairly distant so that Muggles didn't come across it all the time. But I think that people recognise the reality of a lot of children being cloistered together, perhaps, more than they recognise the ambiance of a boarding school. I'm not sure that I'm familiar with that, but I think am familiar with what children are like when they're together."

(112) Monkshood and wolfsbane are the same plant and also known as Aconite.

(113) JK Rowling says she killed Hedwig because it

represented Harry's loss of security and innocence, ending his childhood.

(114) According to the American Library Association, the Harry Potter books are amongst the most banned in America. This is because some religious people and church groups don't like the use of witchcraft and dark magic. JK Rowling (and many fans!) would argue that it's all perfectly harmless though.

(115) Dumbledore was loath to kill the dark wizard Gellert Grindelwald because he had fallen in love with him.

(116) Dumbledore has a scar above his left knee that is a map of the London Underground (subway) system.

(117) JK Rowling says she would choose Professor Lupin to teach her children "because he is kind, clever, and gives very interesting lessons."

(118) In Order of the Phoenix you can deduce cereal boxes for Cheeri-Owls and Pixie Puffs on the breakfast table.

(119) Daniel Radcliffe's stunt double through the first six films, David Holmes, was paralysed from the waist down during the sixth film while working on a flying scene that included an explosion.

(120) Hogwarts has 142 staircases.

(121) JK Rowling feels that Hermione in the books is a very relatable character for girls. "Girls are very tolerant of her because she is not an uncommon female type - the little girl who feels plain and hugely compensates by working very hard and wanting to get everything just so."

(122) Zoe Wanamaker, who played games mistress Madam

Hooch in the first Harry Potter film, did not return in the sequels because her character was written out of the franchise after Wanamaker was openly critical of what she perceived to be low rates of pay for the actors.

(123) In June 2009, the estate of Adrian Jacobs, a children's author who died in 1997, sued Rowling's publishers, Bloomsbury, for £500 million, accusing her of having plagiarised substantial parts of his work The Adventures of Willy the Wizard in the novel Harry Potter and the Goblet of Fire. The claim did not get very far though and a judge said he could see no similarities between the books. This view was shared by Harry Potter fans who were curious enough to read The Adventures of Willy the Wizard.

(124) Cardinal Joseph Ratzinger (Pope Benedict XVI) said the Harry Potter books 'erode Christianity in the soul' of young people and are 'inconsistent with the teachings of the Catholic Church.' Ratzinger said the books were a 'subtle seduction.'.

(125) Robert Pattinson said that he much preferred playing Cedric Diggory in Harry Potter to playing Edward Cullen in the Twilight films.

(126) Of mythology in the books, JK Rowling says - "There's - I'm not trying to work it in, but... If you're writing a book that, I mean, I do do a certain amount of research, and folklore is quite important in the books, so where I'm mentioning a creature or a spell, that people used to believe genuinely worked - of course it didn't - but, you know, it's still a very picturesque and a very comical world in some ways - then I will find out exactly what the words were, and I will find out exactly what the characteristics of that creature or ghost was supposed to be. But I hope that that appears seamlessly. Children often, often ask me how much of the magic is in inverted commas "real" in the books in the sense that did anyone ever believe in this? I would say - a rough proportion -

about a third of the stuff that crops up is stuff that people genuinely used to believe in Britain. Two thirds of it, though, is my invention."

(127) JK Rowling did a lot of work on the Harry Potter books while sitting in the little Elephant House café in Edinburgh.

(128) Ed Tudor-Pole was cast to play Mr Borgin in Chamber of Secrets but had his scenes axed from the film. Tudor-Pole used to present the popular adventure game show The Crystal Maze.

(129) JK Rowling says that Hermione is very dear to her heart. "Hermione is - Hermione, Harry's friend Hermione, is really the brains of the outfit. Anyone who's read the books will know that. And she is a caricature of me at 11. Now, Hermione is very very dear to my heart because of that. I understand her implicitly. She's not exactly like me, because characters always become something very different on the page. So I do feel that I have a female character in there, into whom I've really put a lot of myself."

(130) If you wanted to do a Harry Potter marathon and watch all of the films it would take you about nineteen hours.

(131) Why is the Weasleys' clock set at Mortal Peril? "Mrs Weasley is right," says JK Rowling. "If you don't know what I'm talking about, the Weasleys have a clock in which each of the 9 hands represents a member of the family and they point at things like at work, travelling and so on. Well at the beginning of this book all 9 hands are pointing at mortal peril. Mrs Weasley is right, she hopes that everyone is now in danger and she is correct. Well if the deaf eaters had clocks their hands wouldn't point at mortal peril. And the Weasley are what are called blood traitors; in other words they are pure blood but don't act that way. They consort and like muggles. Therefore they are in the firing line, they would not

be among Voldemort's favourite people?"

(132) Harry Potter producer David Heyman says that, when he was attached to the first film as director, Steven Spielberg wanted to cast Haley Joel Osment (then a successful American child actor) as Harry Potter.

(133) It is estimated that around 16,000 boys were looked at before Daniel Radcliffe was cast as Harry Potter.

(134) JK Rowling has said that Daniel, Rupert, and Emma were all more attractive in the films than how she imagined of her trio of 'geeky' characters.

(135) When they were casting for the first Harry Potter film, the casting director and producer trawled through schools in Britain looking for children to audition. When they got to Emma Watson's school she originally had no interest in doing an audition but was persuaded by her teacher to do one. She was the last girl to audition that day - and ended up being cast in the film!

(136) In 1999, an American author named Nancy Stouffer claimed that JK Rowling had borrowed from her 1984 works 'The Legend of Rah and the Muggles' and 'Larry Potter and His Best Friend Lilly'. However, the court case that followed rejected Stouffer's claims.

(137) JK Rowling says that she pictures Hogwarts in her imagination like this - 'A huge, rambling, quite scary-looking castle, with a jumble of towers and battlements. Like the Weasley's house, it isn't a building that Muggles could build, because it is supported by magic.'

(138) The first book in the Harry Potter series is a fairly concise 76,944 words.

(139) James Sirius Potter's first day at Hogwarts was in 2015.

(140) Daniel Radcliffe got through 160 pairs of prop spectacles during the course of the film series.

(141) The filming location for the Hogwarts interior in the films is the Alnwick Castle in Northumberland.

(142) All the food you see in the great hall scenes of the first Harry Potter movie is real food. The only problem was that with the hot studio lights it tended to smell in the end!

(143) Richard Harris said he only agreed to play Dumbledore because his granddaughter said she'd never speak to him again if he turned the part down.

(144) Hugh Grant was originally cast as Gilderoy Lockhart but had a scheduling conflict with another film he was contracted to.

(145) In 2004, Andy Norfolk, of the Pagan Federation, in response to silly tabloid newspaper claims that Harry Potter fans were becoming involved in witchcraft, said - "In response to increased inquiries coming from youngsters we established a youth officer. It is quite probably linked to things like Harry Potter, Sabrina the Teenage Witch and Buffy the Vampire Slayer. Every time an article on witchcraft or paganism appears, we have a huge surge in calls, mostly from young girls."

(146) The radish earrings worn by Luna Lovegood were made by Evanna Lynch.

(147) Lucius having long hair was an invention of actor Jason Isaacs. "I went to the set, and they had this idea of me wearing a pinstripe suit, short black-and-white hair. I was slightly horrified. He was a racist, a eugenicist. There's no way he

would cut his hair like a Muggle, or dress like a Muggle. In order to keep the hair straight, I had to tip my head back, so I was looking down my nose at everyone. There was 50 percent of the character. I asked for a walking stick, which [Chamber of Secrets director] Chris Columbus first thought was because I had something wrong with my leg. I explained I wanted it as an affectation so I can pull my wand out [of the cane]."

(148) You can now buy a Harry Potter Hogwarts 3,000-Piece Jigsaw Puzzle from Entertainment Earth. The picture you have create is described in the following way - 'As you gaze across the Black Lake, you see the Hogwarts School of Witchcraft and Wizardry rising in all its splendor.'

(149) Gloucester Cathedral was used for some exterior scenes set at Hogwarts.

(150) The cast in the films was told that the Honeydukes chocolate and sweets were not really edible. In reality they were - it was a trick to stop the actors from eating the props!

(151) Over six-hundred school uniforms were needed for the films.

(152) All the potions drunk by characters in the films were soup in reality.

(153) Why did JK Rowling have people close to Harry die in the books? "When you have a hero who is growing up and growing to fulfil a certain destiny, which Harry now is, the ruthless answer is it is much more interesting for him to do that alone. So in terms of your story and your plot and also when you are trying to show the journey of a child into a man really which is what Harry is, the next book he is going to come of age within the wizarding world, so legally actually a man, that is a dramatic and poignant way of showing that journey is to strip him of the people closest to him."

(154) Emma Watson says she ended up doing eight auditions before she was cast.

(155) Daniel Radcliffe says the Potter films were like his 'acting school' and that he slowly got better as they went on.

(156) The moving staircases of Hogwarts in the films were a combination of one real staircase and a tiny model of multiple staircases.

(157) Harry's middle name is James.

(158) The shooting location for Hagrid's Hut and its surroundings is Clachaig Gully.

(159) Four different cats played Hermione's pet, Crookshanks, in the films.

(160) Hermione's middle name is Jane.

(161) The curse used to kill Harry's parents, Avada Kedavra, derives from a phrase in Aramaic Abhadda kedhabhra, which means to disappear like this world.

(162) Comic book historian Michael Mallory pointed out the similarities between Hogwarts School for Witchcraft and Wizarry and Professor Charles Xavier's "Xavier School for Gifted Youngsters" in Marvel Comics X-Men (where those with the X-gene are taken in and taught to control their powers with a possible view to becoming X-Men themselves one day). "Think about [the comic] clad in traditional British university robes and pointy hats, castles and trains, and the image that springs to mind is Hogwarts School for Witchcraft and Wizard[ry], with Dumbledore, Voldemort and the class struggle between wizards and muggles." The X-Men are a superhero team are made up of humans born with the "X-

gene". This gene gives them unique powers and abilities but it also makes them feared by ordinary humans. Those with the X-gene are known as "mutants" and the prejudice they face often holds a mirror to our own reality. Racism, homophobia, McCarthy style Witch Hunts. A general fear of diversity and anyone that might be different. One can argue that the themes of prejudice against anyone seeming to be different are also a key subtext of Harry Potter.

(163) Dementors, the deadly phantoms that guard Azkaban Prison, represent depression and were based on JK Rowling's own experiences of the condition.

(164) The Weasley's Wizard Wheezes store took three months to build for the film series.

(165) JK Rowling says the inspiration for Moaning Myrtle was "the frequent presence of a crying girl in communal bathrooms, especially at the parties and discos of my youth. This does not seem to happen in male bathrooms."

(166) Deathly Hallows sold eleven million copies on its first day of release.

(167) Tom Felton says he hadn't read any of the Harry Potter books before he auditioned to play Draco.

(168) When Harry Potter and the Prisoner of Azkaban was due to be published, the publishers asked for the book to be released when schools were closed for the holidays because they were worried that children might play truant to go and buy it!

(169) Hermione was very nearly named 'Hermione Puckle'.

(170) It is estimated that someone begins a reading a Harry Potter every thirty seconds somewhere in the world.

(171) So many props were used in the Harry Potter films series that it took five warehouses to store them all.

(172) Lacock Abbey in Wiltshire was used to depict the Hogwarts corridors in the films.

(173) JK Rowling says that her perfect job in the wizarding world would be creating spell books.

(174) Peeves the Poltergeist appears in the books but not the films.

(175) The late British comedian and actor Rik Mayall was cast as Peeves in the first film but his scenes were not used. Mayall said that he made the children laugh too much so it was difficult to find a useable take! "I got sent off the set because every time I tried to do a bit of acting, all the lads who were playing the school kids kept getting the giggles, they kept corpsing, so they threw me off. Well, they asked me to do it with my back to them and they still laughed. So they asked me to do it around the other side of the cathedral and shout my lines, but they still laughed so they said they'd do my lines with someone else. So then I did a little bit of filming, then I went home and I got the money. That's significant. Then a month later, they said: 'Er, Rik, we're sorry about this, but you're not in the film. We've cut you out of the film.' But I still got the money. So that is the most exciting film I've ever been in, because I got the oodle and I wasn't in it. Fantastic."

(176) JK Rowling says that she doesn't like sport and Quidditch was her attempt to create a fictional sport that even she might like to watch.

(177) Seven different owls played Hedwig in the films.

(178) Canterbury Cathedral in Kent turned down a request to

be used as one of the doubles for Hogwarts when asked by the film studio.

(179) When Arthur Weasley takes Harry to the Ministry of Magic they must first dial a secret code into a telephone keypad. He enters the number 62442. The letters underneath those numbers on a standard mobile phone spell out the word "magic".

(180) The director Alfonso Cuarón gave the actors in Prisoner of Azkaban permission to wear their Hogwarts uniforms in any way they liked. He felt this made the characters more realistic.

(181) JK Rowling gave Harry Potter spectacles because she wanted to make him seem vulnerable and not superhuman.

(182) Emma Watson was known as 'one-take-Watson' on the Harry Potter set and always became irritated when a scene required multiple takes!

(183) JK Rowling wrote down five pages worth of names before deciding on the word Quidditch.

(184) Dumbledore's full name is Albus Percival Wulfric Brian Dumbledore.

(185) Emma Watson need hair extensions to film Deathly Hallows because she had short hair in real life at the time.

(186) The Goblet of Fire film was going to be split up into two parts at one point.

(187) Daniel Radcliffe broke a lot of wands on the set of the films because he would use them as drumsticks between takes.

(188) Before filming began on Harry Potter and the Prisoner of Azkaban, lead actors Daniel Radcliffe, Rupert Grint and Emma Watson were asked to write autobiographical essays about their characters. Radcliffe wrote one page and Emma Watson wrote ten. Rupert Grint didn't deliver his essay. When questioned why, he said, "I'm Ron. Ron wouldn't do it."

(189) Because there were so many young children on the set of the early Potter films, a full-time dentist had to be hired by the studio due to all the teeth that were falling out!

(190) Emma Watson's studio contract expired after Harry Potter and the Order of the Phoenix. She decided not to leave because she didn't want to see someone else take over the role of Hermione.

(191) Fifteen thousand girls were looked at for the part of Luna Lovegood.

(192) Rupert Grint says he is absolutely terrified of spiders in real-life.

(193) The young actors in the Harry Potter films were banned from participating in contact or extreme sports while under contract to the studio.

(194) The American wizard body is the Magical Congress of the United States of America and the boss is Samuel G Quahog.

(195) JK Rowling doesn't like cats. She said she'd put them in Room 101.

(196) The name of Professor McGonagall's cat double is Mrs P Head.

(197) Helen McCrory was originally cast as Bellatrix Lestrange

but had to decline the part when she became pregnant. She was replaced by Helena Bonham Carter.

(198) Helen McCrory was later cast as Narcissa Malfoy.

(199) The production of Harry Potter and the Order of the Phoenix took a two month break so that Daniel Radcliffe and Emma Watson could sit school exams.

(200) JK Rowling always planned Harry Potter to be a long saga and had a story arc planned right from the beginning. "I planned it to be a series from the very start, and when I first met my British editor face-to-face, I knew that, at some point during that first lunch meeting, I would have to say, very tentatively, 'Do you think you might want a sequel . . . or two? Because, basically, I have planned seven.' Bits of some of them were already written even then, so I kept thinking, please want more. Thank God, after the first course, he turned to me and said, 'So, obviously we're thinking sequels.' And I was so relieved. I think I said something like, 'Well, yes, I think I can probably manage one -- or six.' And he was fine with that plan. There are a couple of unexplained questions at the end of each of the books, so the story can go on."

(201) The producers say that one of the reasons why they cast Daniel Radcliffe was that he seemed like an 'old soul' in a young body.

(202) Harry Potter And The Deathly Hallows Part 2 had the biggest ever weekend opening box-office for a film at that time.

(203) In the Yule Ball scenes in Goblet of Fire, we only see Harry Potter from the waist up. This is because Daniel Radcliffe didn't have time for dance lessons and so didn't know the footwork and moves for this sequence.

(204) Rob Reiner and Tim Robbins were other names considered when a director was needed for the first Harry Potter film. Reiner, who directed the cult classics The Princess Bride and Stand By Me, didn't want to commit to spending so much time away from his home in America and so declined.

(205) In Quidditch, penalties can be awarded to teams by the referee. A single Chaser may take the penalty by flying from the central circle towards the scoring area. The opposing team's Keeper may attempt to stop the shot being scored, but all other players must not interfere (it is unknown if the Seeker may still attempt to catch the Snitch while a penalty is being attempted).

(206) Rupert Grint says that he was so young when he made the first Harry Potter film that he can't remember what life was like before that.

(207) A first edition of Harry Potter and the Philosopher's Stone once sold for $90,000. Before you get excited and start trawling for your own first edition of this book to put on Ebay, the copy in question was exceptionally rare in that it had typos and an illustration of a wizard on the back cover that never featured in any other copies.

(208) Chris Columbus did not direct the third Harry Potter film because he didn't feel he had the energy to go through the process of making such a big film again.

(209) The Malfoys' last name derives from the Latin term maleficus. It means wicked, accursed, evil.

(210) JK Rowling says that when she first sent out of the manuscript and synopsis of the first Harry Potter book to publishers, one rejection came back so quickly that they couldn't possibly have read it. Whoever was responsible for that rejection made a huge mistake!

(211) The cry of the Mandrake is deadly to anyone who hears it.

(212) Daniel Radcliffe was in the bath when news came in that he'd been cast as Harry Potter. By way of celebration he was allowed to stay up thirty minutes past his usual bedtime.

(213) A 2011 survey reported that a third of all American adults aged 18 to 34 had read at least one of the Harry Potter books.

(214) Kate Winslet was offered the role of Ravenclaw's Grey Lady, Helena Ravenclaw. Winslet says that, much to her regret, her agent turned the part down without consulting her.

(215) Daniel Radcliffe and Rupert Grint think that Hermione's cat in the films wasn't very attractive. Emma Watson disagreed and thought it was a lovely cat.

(216) Moly is a very helpful plant that can be eaten to counteract enchantments.

(217) The Harry Potter books have sold over 500 million copies.

(218) The Harry Potter books have been translated into over 80 languages.

(219) At the end of the closing credits for Goblet of Fire, a message reads - No dragons were harmed in the making of this movie.

(220) JK Rowling says that folklore was a big influence on Harry Potter. "Folktales are generally told for a reason. They're ways for children to explore their darkest fears. That's why they endure - that you have archetypes, you have a

wicked stepmother, this threatening figure who should be nurturing and who isn't. So these images crop up again and again and again... If you read Grimm's fairytales in the original, they are very brutal and they are frightening. And in fact, I think, more frightening than anything I've written so far. I mean, children being murdered. There are horrible things. But this is centuries back, and I don't think children have changed that much. I think they still have the same worries, and fears."

(221) Daniel Radcliffe is only 5'5 tall.

(222) Flobberworm mucus is a very useful potion thickener.

(223) Emma Watson was embarrassed by the scene in Chamber of Secrets where she has to hug Harry and Ron so the director allowed her to hug Daniel very briefly and then shake Rupert Grint's hand.

(224) The Knight Bus had to be heavily weighted to stop it from toppling over.

(225) Rupert Grint said it was very strange shooting the scene where Ron and Hermione kiss. "I've known Emma since I was nine and she's like my sister," he said.

(226) Gillyweed is a magical plant that allows the user to survive underwater.

(227) Emma Watson says it was very difficult to adjust to fame at such a young age. When the Potter movies became big business she had to have minders and bodyguards.

(228) Daniel Radcliffe was allergic to the first pair of spectacles he had to wear as Harry Potter.

(229) Science fiction author Orson Scott Card of Ender's Game

fame, seemed to think that JK Rowling was influenced by his own cult novel. "A young kid growing up in an oppressive family situation suddenly learns that he is one of a special class of children with special abilities, who are to be educated in a remote training facility where student life is dominated by an intense game played by teams flying in midair, at which this kid turns out to be exceptionally talented and a natural leader. He trains other kids in unauthorised extra sessions, which enrages his enemies, who attack him with the intention of killing him; but he is protected by his loyal, brilliant friends and gains strength from the love of some of his family members. He is given special guidance by an older man of legendary accomplishments who previously kept the enemy at bay. He goes on to become the crucial figure in a struggle against an unseen enemy who threatens the whole world."

(230) The animatronic Phoenix used for Fawkes seemed so lifelike that Richard Harris thought it was a real bird at first.

(231) Chris Columbus said that the Harry Potter film franchise was very fortunate that Daniel, Rupert, and Emma did not age awkwardly (which can happen with child actors - they can sometimes end up looking very different as teenagers).

(232) Celebrity Harry Potter fans include Selena Gomez and Margot Robie.

(233) Daniel Radcliffe and Rupert Grint say they both had a crush on Emma Watson when they began making the Potter films together.

(234) Ian McKellen says he was approached to play Dumbledore when Richard Harris passed away. Nothing came of this though and Michael Gambon got the part in the end. McKellen had already played a famous wizard with his role as Gandalf in the Lord of the Rings films.

(235) Asked if Tolkien was an influence on Harry Potter, JK Rowling said that she read Lord of the Rings when she was twenty but had never picked the book up again.

(236) Daniel Radcliffe had lost interest in acting when the first Harry Potter film was casting and didn't want to be involved. It took a personal plea from the producer David Heyman to persuade him to audition for the part of Harry.

(237) Daniel Radcliffe had to shave the bottom of his leg for a scene in the second film where Harry puts a sock on. It was felt that his legs were too hairy for a twelve year-old character!

(238) The actors who appear in all eight Harry Potter movies are - Daniel Radcliffe, Rupert Grint, Emma Watson, Robbie Coltrane, Alan Rickman, Tom Felton, Matthew Lewis, Devon Murray, James and Oliver Phelps, Josh Herdman, Warwick Davis, and Geraldine Somerville.

(239) The producers (and one might venture fans too) felt that while Chris Columbus did solid work in establishing Harry Potter on the big screen his departure was a blessing in disguise because gave the franchise a fresh creative sensibility that was bolder and darker. One could argue that the films made after Chris Columbus were more interesting.

(240) Hero Fiennes-Tiffin, who played the young Tom Riddle, is Voldemort actor Ralph Fiennes' nephew.

(241) Warner Brothers had to re-sign their main cast again on Harry Potter And The Order Of The Phoenix because the principal actors were only signed for four films at the start of the franchise.

(242) Custard tarts are mentioned in the Harry Potter books. This is a treat which dates back to Medieval times. It is a pastry consisting of an outer pastry crust filled with egg

custard and then baked. Custard tarts are still a popular staple in the fresh cakes sections of British supermarkets.

(243) Expecto Patronum is Latin for 'I await a guardian'.

(244) JK Rowling says she finds religious criticism of the Harry Potter books strange because she goes to church herself and believes in life after death.

(245) Emma Watson tripped and fell during a take on Goblet of Fire when Hermione had to walk down some stairs for the ball.

(246) The scar was applied to Radcliffe's forehead by the make-up department a total of 5,800 times throughout the film series.

(247) In the first book in the series, Harry Potter is only 11 years old.

(248) When Draco tells Harry in the film series that he is surprised he can read, this insult was improvised by Tom Felton.

(249) The Black family tree contains over 70 names and was written by JK Rowling.

(250) Starbucks produced a Harry Potter inspired Butterbeer Frappuccino. The recipe is thought to be a Creme Frappuccino base, caramel syrup, toffee nut syrup, caramel drizzle.

(251) JK Rowling says she finds girls who love Draco a little bit worrying. "It amuses me. It honestly amuses me. People have been waxing lyrical [in letters] about Draco Malfoy, and I think that's the only time when it stopped amusing me and started almost worrying me. I'm trying to clearly distinguish between Tom Felton, who is a good looking young boy, and

Draco, who, whatever he looks like, is not a nice man. It's a romantic, but unhealthy, and unfortunately all too common delusion of — delusion, there you go — of girls, and you will know this, that they are going to change someone. And that persists through many women's lives, till their death bed, and it is uncomfortable and unhealthy and it actually worried me a little bit, to see young girls swearing undying devotion to this really imperfect character, because there must be an element in there, that 'I'd be the one who [changes him].' I mean, I understand the psychology of it, but it is pretty unhealthy. So, a couple of times I have written back, possibly quite sharply, saying [Laughter], 'You want to rethink your priorities here.'"

(252) Harry Potter doesn't cast a spell in the entirety of the first film.

(253) There were some bizarre stories in 2003 that Russian lawyers were going to sue Warner Brothers because they believed that Dobby the elf was based on Russia's long standing leader Vladimir Putin!

(254) The Bodleian Libraries in Oxford doubled for the Hogwarts library in the films.

(255) Harry Melling, who plays Dudley Dursely, in the films, lost so much weight between the second and third films that he was nearly axed from the franchise! In the end he had to wear a fake fatsuit.

(256) In the Potter books, Harry nearly breaks a tooth on Hagrid's rock cakes. Rock cakes in reality are supposed to be soft and rather like scones.

(257) In a game of Quidditch, contact is allowed, but a player may not seize hold of another player's broomstick or any part of their anatomy.

(258) Daniel Radcliffe has embraced many eclectic roles since Harry Potter. He said this was not a conscious attempt to escape from his Potter image but more because he is naturally drawn to strange projects.

(259) Ian Brown makes a cameo in Harry Potter And The Prisoner Of Azkaban as a wizard in The Leaky Cauldron. Ian Brown was the lead singer of pop group The Stone Roses.

(260) They used CGI to depict the possessed Harry's eyes in the film series because Daniel Radcliffe is allergic to contact lenses.

(261) The five-digit code in the red telephone booth for entrance to the Ministry of Magic is 6-2-4-4-2.

(262) Some fans of the Harry Potter books think that the other friends of the main trio get short shrift in the film series. This is perhaps an understandable and unavoidable consequence of a book having more time and space to develop supporting characters than a film.

(263) Starbucks produced Harry Potter inspired Pumpkin Juice. If you want to try this at home the best recipe is to mix pumpkin juice with apple juice and add some ice.

(264) Emma Watson asked the props department to add more books to the scene in Harry Potter And The Deathly Hallows Part 1 where we see Hermione's bedroom.

(265) Verne Troyer was one of the few American actors to grace the Harry Potter films. He played Griphook the goblin - though his voice was dubbed.

(266) The underwater scenes in Harry Potter And The Goblet Of Fire left Daniel Radcliffe with an ear infection.

(267) Fourteen Ford Anglia cars were wrecked during the filming of the scene where Harry and Ron crash into the tree.

(268) Butterbeer in the films is really the soft-drink Orange J20 topped up with foam.

(269) One could argue that Harry Potter is influenced by Star Wars, a project which had its roots in Joseph Campbell's writings on legend and myths. Both Harry Potter and Luke Skywalker lead dull lives until their true destiny is revealed. The 'dark side' is a theme of both films - as are the mentor figures who train our heroes.

(270) Crumpets are mentioned in the Potter books. A crumpet is a small griddle cake made from an unsweetened batter of water or milk, flour and yeast. Crumpets have holes in the top so that the butter seeps down. They make a delicious alternative to toast.

(271) Emma Watson said she had a crush on Tom Felton when they were making the films.

(272) There is a potion used to develop photographs in the Wizarding World and it is this specific potion that makes images come to life.

(273) The ingredients in Polyjuice Potion are Lacewing flies, leeches, powdered Bicorn horn, knotgrass, fluxweed, shredded Boomslang skin, and something of the person you want to turn into.

(274) JK Rowling says that twelve publishing houses rejected Harry Potter and the Philosopher's Stone.

(275) The anagram for Severus Snape is Persues Evans.

(276) Shepherd's pie is mentioned in the Harry Potter books. This is a well known dish in Britain and Ireland. It is minced meat, carrots, and onions in gravy topped with mashed potato and then baked in a dish until the top has gone crispy. You can easily make a vegetarian Shepherd's pie too.

(277) Terry Gilliam (of Time Bandits and Monty Python fame) was JK Rowling's choice to direct the first Harry Potter film. Gilliam was on a shortlist of potential directors but the studio did not want him. "I was the perfect person to do Harry Potter," Gilliam complained. "I remember leaving the meeting, getting in my car, and driving for about two hours along Mulholland Drive just so angry. I mean, Chris Columbus' versions are terrible. Just dull. Pedestrian."

(278) Despite his anger at being rejected, Gilliam later seemed to be express relief that he wasn't chosen. "That was one of my lucky moments," he told Total Film magazine. "I would have gone crazy. It's a factory, working on Harry Potter. It is. The studios are staking everything on the success of those movies. It was way too expensive. Too much at stake. So they [the studio bosses] interfere."

(279) The inscription around the Mirror of Erised is 'Erised stra ehru oyt ube cafru oyt on wohsi' which is 'I show not your face, but your heart's desire' spelt backwards.

(280) Domhnall Gleeson, who played Bill Weasley, is the son of Mad-Eye Moody actor Brendan Gleeson.

(281) For the Knight Bus scenes in the films, the bus was driven at normal speed while the cars around it went super slow. This was then speeded up in the editing room to give the effect of a magical bus.

(282) JK Rowling, more or less, based Hermione on herself at the same age.

(283) Alan Parker was one of the names considered when they were searching for a director to take charge of the first Harry Potter film. Parker had worked with young casts before on films like Bugsy Malone and Fame. However, he wasn't really interested and declined to get involved. "While that would have made me extremely rich today, my problem with it was that I didn't like it, I didn't understand it and I wasn't interested in it."

(284) Nigel Wolpert (William Melling) is an invention for the films. He seems to be an amalgam of Harry-stanning siblings Colin and Dennis Creevey.

(285) The Elder Wand is the only wand to contain hair from the Thestral.

(286) When the last scene on the last day of the last Harry Potter film wrapped, Daniel Radcliffe did not have time to wallow in sadness or nostalgia. He began work on a play the next day.

(287) A ticket on the Knight Bus with hot chocolate costs 14 sickles.

(288) During a scene on Harry Potter and the Order of the Phoenix, Helena Bonham Carter ruptured Mathew Lewis's eardrum when her character put her wand in his character's ear.

(289) Arthur Weasley was supposed to meet his demise in Harry Potter and the Order of the Phoenix but was replaced with Sirius.

(290) Robbie Coltrane was the first actor to be cast when they made the first film.

(291) In Latin, Bellatrix is a term for a female warrior.

(292) Hermione got her love of otters because JK Rowling loves them.

(293) Spotted Dick is mentioned in Goblet of Fire. This is a suet pudding made with currants or raisins. It's an old fashioned British dessert traditionally served with custard.

(294) Harry Potter reminded some readers of Eva Ibbotson's 1994 children's book The Secret of Platform 13. Both of the books feature King's Cross Station in London. Eva Ibbotson has shrugged off alleged similarities though and said "I would like to shake her [Rowling] by the hand. I think we all borrow from each other as writers."

(295) It is said that, for Chamber of Secrets, Daniel Radcliffe was to be paid £125,000 until the actors' union Equity negotiated a better deal. Radcliffe ended up being paid two million pounds for the film.

(296) Yorkshire Pudding is mentioned in the Harry Potter books. This is a baked pudding made from batter consisting of eggs, flour, and milk or water. Yorkshire Pudding is a common sidedish in Britain. A Yorkshire Pudding made with sausages cooked into it is known as Toad-in-the-Hole. In the United States, Yorkshire puddings are known as Popovers.

(297) Daniel Radcliffe's casting as Harry Potter was aided by the fact that the producers had been impressed by him in an adaptation of Dickens' David Copperfield. One could say there are some interesting parallels between David Copperfield and Harry Potter in that they are both orphans who achieved great things after a difficult start in life.

(298) In Quidditch, players must not stray over the boundary lines of the pitch, although they may fly as high as desired.

The Quaffle must be surrendered to the opposition if any player leaves the boundary (it is unknown what the penalty is if a player on defence leaves the pitch).

(299) JK Rowling says that - "My characters come organically, and they come through this mysterious process no one really understands. They just pop up, or... But they're sometimes inspired by real people."

(300) Surveys suggest that 55% of the readers of YA (young adult) fiction are adults rather than children or teenagers.

(301) When asked what his favorite scene to shoot was, Daniel Radcliffe said - "The first thing that comes to mind, and it's a silly one, but doing all the Gringott's stuff in the last movie with Rupert [Grint] and Helena [Bonham Carter] and Warwick [Davis] and Emma [Watson]. That was like a really fun time. We were all enjoying ourselves in that. It's an action sequence so it was more of a technical challenge than an emotional one."

(302) JK Rowling has admitted that Roald Dahl was an influence on her work. Roald Dahl was a legendary children's author who wrote (amongst others) James and the Giant Peach, Charlie and the Chocolate Factory, Matilda, The Witches, Fantastic Mr Fox, and The BFG.

(303) Some readers think Ursula K. Le Guin's A Wizard of Earthsea was an influence on Harry Potter. This 1968 fantasy novel is set in the fictional archipelago of Earthsea and concerns a young mage named Ged, born in a village on the island of Gont. He displays great power while still a boy and joins the school of wizardry. "I didn't feel she ripped me off, as some people did," Ursula K. Le Guin said of JK Rowling, "though she could have been more gracious about her predecessors. My incredulity was at the critics who found the first book wonderfully original. She has many virtues, but

originality isn't one of them. That hurt."

(304) Eddie Redmayne auditioned to be Tom Riddle in Harry Potter but didn't get the part. He was later cast as Newt Scamander in Fantastic Beasts.

(305) The inspiration for the name Hermione is William Shakespeare's play The Winter's Tale. Hermione is the virtuous and beautiful Queen of Sicilia.

(306) Alan Horn, the president of Warner Bros when the Potter films were first optioned, said that no one there liked Steven Spielberg's idea of mashing up a couple of books into one story and doing it as an animated film.

(307) JK Rowling says that the first book to inspire her as a child was Kenneth Grahame's The Wind in the Willows.

(308) Rupert Grint's favourite book in the series is Harry Potter and the Goblet of Fire.

(309) JK Rowling used to be a teacher.

(310) David Heyman says that when Harry Potter and the Philosopher's Stone reached his office it was put on a pile of scripts and books considered to have low-potential for a film. One of his assistants took it home to read and came back into the office raving about it.

(311) Culpeper's Complete Herbal, which was so influential to JK Rowling when writing Harry Potter, can be purchased online. "It's just the way they wrote about the plants and observed them and tied them planetary movements and so on," said Rowling. "There's such a poetry to it… Even when I didn't really use what they were saying, I found it inspirational, I found the way they talked about these plants inspirational."

(312) The illustrations on the kitchen wall at 4 Privet Drive in the films were made by local children.

(313) When asked who his favourite Harry Potter character was, Daniel Radcliffe said - "Probably Sirius. Like I always loved the character, and then Gary [Oldman]'s portrayal of him I thought was perfect. Or Lupin, really. Any of the characters my dad used to hang out with, other than Wormtail. There was always something about those two I loved a lot."

(314) The entire industry spawned by Harry Potter is said to be worth $25 billion.

(315) Emma Watson had only acted in a few school plays before being cast as Hermione.

(316) Shooting on the film version of Chamber of Secrets started only three days after Philosopher's Stone finished production.

(317) All first-years at Hogwarts must take seven core subjects - Transfiguration, Charms, Potions, History of Magic, Defence Against the Dark Arts, Astronomy and Herbology. Flying lessons (on broomsticks) are also compulsory.

(318) Sticky Toffee Pudding features at the Leaky Cauldron. Sticky toffee pudding is an English dessert consisting of a very moist sponge cake covered in a toffee sauce.

(319) Harry Potter reminded some readers of Groosham Grange - a 1988 book by Anthony Horowitz. The book is about a mistreated teenager who ends up at a boarding school for wizards and witches.

(320) Coconut ice is mentioned in the Harry Potter books.

Coconut ice is a British confectionery made with grated desiccated coconut, condensed milk and sugar.

(321) Stephen Fry, who narrated the Harry Potter audiobooks in Britain, has noted the similarities between Harry Potter and Tom Brown's Schooldays by Thomas Hughes. "Harry Potter – a boy who arrives in this strange school to board for the first time and makes good, solid friends and also enemies who use bullying and unfair tactics, then is ambiguous about whether or not he is going to be good or bad. His pluck and his endeavour, loyalty, good nature and bravery are the things that carry him through – and that is the story of Tom Brown's Schooldays."

(322) When he was asked if he'd be interested in directing the first Harry Potter film, Alan Parker told the producers they should be talking to Terry Gilliam!

(323) The rock band at the Yule Ball In Goblet of Fire is made up of real musicians from Pulp and Radiohead.

(324) Over 25,000 items of clothing and costuming were used during the Harry Potter film franchise.

(325) The Harry Potter films were based at Leavesden Studios in Hertfordshire. This used to be a disused Aerodrome and was turned into a film studio in the 1990s to make the Bond film GoldenEye.

(326) The Harry Potter universe suggests that the great wizard Merlin went to Hogwarts.

(327) 12,000 prop books were required for the film series.

(328) Tom Felton said he was rather intimidated by Alan Rickman at first because Rickman was a method actor who completely inhabited the role of Snape.

(329) Michael Gambon was definitely not a method actor. He used to wear his street clothes underneath his Dumbledore costume.

(330) Although Hermione is the oldest of the central trio in the books, Emma Watson was the youngest of the three main actors in the films.

(331) An outbreak of lice occurred among the child cast members during the filming of Harry Potter and the Chamber of Secrets.

(332) JK Rowling says she is a fan of the Narnia books by CS Lewis. One can see the influence of these books on Harry Potter.

(333) Daniel Radcliffe says he was disappointed that Nearly Headless Nick's party from the book Chamber of Secrets wasn't in the film version.

(334) Harry Potter producer David Heyman said that one actor he would love to have had in the films was Daniel Day-Lewis.

(335) Chris Colmbus had to battle the studio to do full justice to Dumbledore's elaborate office. The studio didn't want to give him the extra money he needed at first to create this intricate set.

(336) The underwater set built for Goblet of Fire could hold 50,000 litres of water.

(337) M. Night Shyamalan wanted to direct a Harry Potter film and was under consideration a few times but it never happened in the end.

(338) JK Rowling is a true rags to riches story. At one point she was a single mother on government welfare before she sold the first book.

(339) Dragon blood can be a surprisingly useful oven cleaner.

(340) JK Rowling thinks that Ron and Hermione will definitely end up needing marriage counselling.

(341) Rupert Grint said he got off to bad start in the films when he dropped a milkshake in Alan Rickman's car.

(342) Emma Watson was born in France but grew up in London and Oxfordshire.

(343) The scenes in the movie franchise where Ballatrix tortures Hermione had to heavily edited in the United States to avoid the film getting a higher cinema certificate.

(344) The Sword of Gryffindor used in the film series was a real sword that was found at an auction.

(345) The young cast members say that Alan Rickman was very generous in giving them advice about their careers and the acting profession.

(346) Three different owls played Hedwig in the films.

(347) The Harry Potter books were instrumental in making it more commonplace for children's books to be longer. It was sometimes assumed that children didn't have the attention span to read a full length book but this was patently not the case.

(348) If you want to be admitted to Hogwarts you must be from Britain or Ireland.

(349) The first film in the Harry Potter franchise had the most mixed reviews. Fans and critics would probably agree that the films got better and more interesting as the series went on.

(350) Some Harry Potter fans quite like the idea of the books being adapted into a faithful TV show or miniseries one day. This longer format would allow plot threads and supporting characters to be fleshed out more than they were in the films.

(351) Third year students at Hogwarts must take: Transfiguration, Charms, Potions, History of Magic, Defence Against the Dark Arts, Astronomy, Herbology, and two or more electives.

(352) Daniel Radcliffe's original contract for Harry Potter stipulated that he must be available to make the films in Hollywood. As it turned out they were made in Britain and he didn't have to travel.

(353) Ron Weasley's Patronus is a Jack Russell Terrier.

(354) JK Rowling nearly gave Draco Malfoy the name Draco Spungen.

(355) Rosamund Pike turned down the part of Rita Skeeter.

(356) Hermione's parents are dentists.

(357) JK Rowling's favourite mythical creature is a phoenix.

(358) JK Rowling says that the death of her mother informed the themes of loss that are apparent in the Harry Potter books.

(359) Daniel Radcliffe took home a pair of Harry Potter's glasses as a memento when the films ended.

(360) JK Rowling sold the film rights for £1.5 million. A

bargain for the studio in hindsight considering how much the films made.

(361) No two wands in the film series were ever alike.

(362) The Harry Potter books are credited with making YA fiction big business again. The Hunger Games and Twilight books were huge hits and, like Harry Potter, an example of books which were primarily aimed at younger readers but could be enjoyed by adults.

(363) The menu at Hogwarts probably wouldn't impress a nutritionist with its rich puddings and sweets!

(364) Emma Watson said that her favourite prop in the film franchise was the Time Turner.

(365) Tom Felton auditioned to play Harry in the first film but was given the part of Draco Malfoy in the end.

(366) The scenes of 4 Privet Drive were shot in a real street but when they lost permission to shoot here in later films they simply built a replica street that was identical!

(367) When Emma Watson was introduced to the kids from (the movie of) Stephen King's IT, she thought they were the Stranger Things kids. She'd obviously never watched Stranger Things or Stephen King's IT!

(368) JK Rowling says it is possible that the name Hogwarts derives from her looking at a hogwort plant in Kew Gardens while in New York. The name just stuck in her head.

(369) An intricate model of Hogwarts was used in the films although later on more CGI was deployed to depict the school.

(370) The food in the Harry Potter books is very anachronistic at times. Few people in Britain actually eat things like steak & kidney pudding, spotted dick, and blancmange anymore.

(371) JK Rowling does not believe in magic. "Not in the slightest. Children ask me, of course, "do you believe in magic?" and I've always said "no, I don't". I believe in different kinds of magic. There's a kind of magic that happens when you pick up a wonderful book, and it lives with you for the rest of your life. That is my kind of magic. There's magic in friendship and in beauty. Metaphorical magic."

(372) The Harry Potter books have remarkable international appeal. The Potter craze hit places as far afield as Japan, Germany, and Australia.

(373) Drew Barrymore, a big Harry Potter fan, was very disappointed when her cameo in the first film ended up on the cutting room floor.

(374) As a memento from his time making the films, Rupert Grint took home the Number 4 Privet Drive sign.

(375) Evanna Lynch was allowed to design some of her Luna Lovegood costumes in the films.

(376) Hagrid is allergic to cats.

(377) In the film version of Goblet of Fire, Hermione wears a pink dress to the Yule Ball rather than a blue one (as in the book). This was because the costume designer thought that blue didn't suit Emma Watson and the set background was also blue so it would have been difficult for the dress to be noticed.

(378) One of the stipulations that JK Rowling made when she sold the film rights was that any films had to be based on the

stories in the books. She didn't want someone to just get the rights to the Harry Potter characters and then make up their own story.

(379) In Chamber of Secrets, you can see a picture of Gandalf from Lord of the Rings in Dumbledore's study if you look fast enough.

(380) You can, should you wish, buy a Harry Potter And The Prisoner Of Azkaban Top Trumps Card Game.

(381) JK Rowling's publisher suggested Harry's creator use the name JK Rowling so male readers wouldn't know she was a woman. Her real name is Joanne Rowling.

(382) In the Harry Potter books, red represents good and green represents evil.

(383) Voldemort's wand is made of yew. The yew is one of the oldest species of tree in Europe. This has made it a symbol of death and doom.

(384) 2016 saw the release of a play called Harry Potter and the Cursed Child - written by Jack Thorne based on an original story by JK Rowling, John Tiffany, and Thorne.

The story begins nineteen years after the events of the 2007 novel Harry Potter and the Deathly Hallows and has Harry Potter now Head of the Department of Magical Law Enforcement at the Ministry of Magic. The play got solid reviews although an unquantifiable number of Harry Potter fans thought it played like fanfiction and had a number of plot holes.

(385) There is a clear visual resemblance in the imagery of Sue Townsend's Adrian Mole and Harry Potter. Gian Sammarco, in the 1980s Adrian Mole TV show, looks remarkably like

Harry Potter. It might be pure coincidence - although JK Rowling did tweet when Sue Townsend died to say how much she had enjoyed the Adrian Mole books.

(386) Jim Dale narrated the Harry Potter audiobooks in the United States. Jim Dale is well known in Britain because of his appearances in the vintage and beloved Carry On series of comedy films.

(387) Sweets (candy) in the Harry Potter universe include Bertie Bott's Every Flavour Beans, Drooble's Best Blowing Gum, chocolate frogs, pumpkin pasties, cauldron cakes, Liquorice Wands, Pepper Imps, chocolate balls full of strawberry mousse and clotted cream, Sugar Quills, tooth flossing string mints, Jelly Slugs, nougat, toffees, Fizzing Whizbees, ice mice, peppermint toads, blood flavoured lollipops, Cockroach Cluster, fudge flies, Acid Pops, sherbet balls.

(388) Professor McGonagall was a great Quidditch player but a bad fall in her last year at Hogwarts forced her to stop playing.

(389) JK Rowling has not ruled out writing more Harry Potter books but has some doubts that readers would want Harry as a mature character. The obvious appeal of Harry Potter is that it is a coming of age story about a young person.

(390) Before Hogwarts students reach the age of 11, they are homeschooled by their parents if they're from a wizarding household or educated in the muggle school system.

(391) JK Rowling says that Hermione was originally going to have a younger sister but she simply didn't have the time to write this character into the story in the end.

(392) It is probably fair to say that out of the child actors (they

were children in the early films at least) in Harry Potter, Emma Watson is the one who went on to become the biggest star.

(393) Daniel Radcliffe says, that as regards to staying grounded in the midst of young fame and media attention - "I would attribute it to my parents and also to the crew of the Potter films, who were very good at treating us like kids rather than as actors, as they should have done. But yeah, it's hard to say what it comes down to. I think also when you grow up in the media, you get a very clear sense of how crazy the media is. It was insane. And I think when you see that perspective that we all saw at very young ages, you do get an extra level of awareness maybe."

(394) Richard Harris passed away a few weeks before the second film came out.

(395) Emma Watson seems to have gone out of her way to avoid franchises since Harry Potter. She's never been in a superhero film or anything like that.

(396) JK Rowling says her favourite children's book is The Little White Horse by Elizabeth Goudge.

(397) Rosie O'Donnell lobbied for the part of Molly Weasley in the films but obviously ran foul of the stipulation by JK Rowling that the cast must be British or Irish.

(398) The Wizarding World of Harry Potter theme park in Orlando has served seven different types of Butterbeer.

(399) Concerning the duel between Snape and McGonagall, Alan Rickman said - "Thank God for computer graphics, because holding a wand is not throwing the most threatening thing you can do, and you're pointing it at Dame Maggie Smith, who you grew up worshipping from the cheap seats at

the National Theater, and she's pointing a wand at you. She can arch an eyebrow like nobody. So thank God for the sheets of flame."

(400) JK Rowling says she made the Dursley's house number four because she thinks that number is a jinx.

(401) Slytherin House now contains some non-pure bloods.

(402) JK Rowling thinks the literature is a good way to teach children that life can be difficult sometimes. "And literature is an excellent way, because they have to bring their own imagination to it, so this is something they really participate in, when they create the story inside their own head after reading it on the page. It's a fabulous way to explore those things. Now, I don't set out thinking, this is what they're going to learn in this book, ever. I have a real horror of preaching to anyone, or of trying to make, you know, enormous points. You know, I'm not driven by the need to teach children anything, although those things do come up naturally in the stories, which I think is quite moral. Because it's a battle between good and evil. But I do think, that to pretend to children that life is sanitized and easy, when they already know - they don't need me to tell them - that life can be very difficult. And it's not a bad idea that they meet this in literature."

(403) There are five wizarding schools apart from Hogwarts.

(404) Daniel Radcliffe said that if he had to be in a Hogwarts house it would definitely be Gryffindor.

(405) Lucius Malfoy wanted Draco to attend Durmstrang because of his dislike of Muggle-borns and the family connection to Dark Magic. However, Narcissa didn't like the idea of Draco being so far away.

(406) The Harry Potter books have spent a combined 1,749 weeks on USA TODAY's Best-Selling Books list.

(407) Quidditch began in the 11th century at a place called Queerditch Marsh - absent on muggle maps because wizards have made the place unplottable. Originally it was a crude game played on broomsticks with just the quaffle.

(408) Emma Watson said that the most difficult thing about playing Hermione was that the character talked very fast.

(409) In Quidditch, time out may be called at any time by the Captain of a team. Time out may be extended to two hours if a game has already lasted for more than twelve hours. Failure to return to the pitch after this time will lead to the team being disqualified.

(410) Matthew Lewis and Evvana Lynch would roll bagels across the set to amuse themselves when they didn't have a scene to film.

(411) ESDEVIUM GAMES LTD released a 'Cooperative Deck-Building' Harry Potter board game in 2017. The blurb went like this - 'Play as your favourite characters and defend the wizarding world from evil forces. Enhance your abilities as you build your deck with over 140 cards. Seven successive game adventures offer increasing difficulty as you battle Villains and unlock new abilities, secrets and challenges. Also included are four Hogwarts house dice, game board, over 50 chip pieces, and sorting cards to keep everything organized.'

(412) JK Rowling insisted to the producers that Maggie Smith had to play Minerva McGonagall.

(413) In 2007, JK Rowling was runner up for Time magazine's Person of the Year

(414) The Harry Potter books have been translated into Latin and Ancient Greek.

(415) Why does JK Rowling think Voldemort was referred to as You-Know-Who and He-Who-Must-Not-Be-Named? "It happens many times in history — well, you'll know this because you're that kind of people, but for those who don't, having a taboo on a name is quite common in certain civilizations. In Africa there are tribes where the name is never used. Your name is a sacred part of yourself and you are referred to as the son of so-and-so, the brother of so-and-so, and you're given these pseudonyms, because your name is something that can be used magically against you if it's known. It's like a part of your soul. That's a powerful taboo in many cultures and across many folklores. On a more prosaic note, in the 1950s in London there were a pair of gangsters called the Kray Twins. The story goes that people didn't speak the name Kray. You just didn't mention it. You didn't talk about them, because retribution was so brutal and bloody. I think this is an impressive demonstration of strength, that you can convince someone not to use your name. Impressive in the sense that demonstrates how deep the level of fear is that you can inspire. It's not something to be admired."

(416) JK Rowling says that The Mirror of Erised is one of her favourite chapters in the books.

(417) When Coca-Cola won the rights to use Harry Potter and the Sorcerer's Stone with its products, JK Rowling asked that the company donate $18 million to the US Reading Is Fundamental campaign.

(418) JK Rowling says that - "The wizards represent all that the true muggle most fears: They are plainly outcasts and comfortable with being so. Nothing is more unnerving to the truly conventional than the unashamed misfit!"

(419) The average Hogwarts intake for Muggle-borns is 25%.

(420) Moaning Myrtle was a member of Ravenclaw House.

(421) Harry Potter is described as having longish unruly hair in the books. Daniel Radcliffe rarely has this in the films.

(422) Arithmancy was Hermione Granger's favourite subject at Hogwarts.

(423) Arithmancy is a form of numerology that was developed by ancient Greeks during war times to try to determine and potentially change the outcome of a battle.

(424) Christian Coulson secured the part of Tom Riddle despite being twenty-three years-old. This part was written for someone in their mid-teens.

(425) Many fans and admirers of the Harry Potter books think that the great strength of the series is that JK Rowling had it all mapped out from the start. She knew exactly where the story was going to go in later volumes.

(426) Bonnie Wright was exactly 9 ¾ years old when she started filming Harry Potter and - appropriately enough - her first scene was set on Platform 9 ¾.

(427) JK Rowling says she would be terrible at Quidditch because she doesn't like heights.

(428) Harry Potter is the bestselling book series of all time.

(429) Apple pie is mentioned in the Harry Potter books. Though much loved in America, apple pie was invented in England and dates back to the time of Chaucer. The first apple pie recipe was recorded in 1381!

(430) Harry's favourite spell is of course Expecto patronum!

(431) JK Rowling thought that Robbie Coltrane was perfect for Hagrid because he was cuddly but with a slight hint of menace!

(432) In 2003, members of the Jesus Non-Denominational Church in Greenville, Michigan, burned Harry Potter books on a fire in protest as what they saw as 'evil' themes in the stories.

(433) JK Rowling likes the fact that Harry isn't perfect and makes mistakes. "It's not a bad idea that they can see a character who is - I mean, Harry is a human boy, he makes mistakes, but I think he came as a very noble character, he's a brave character and he strives to do the right thing. And to see a fictional character dealing with those sort of things, I think can be very very helpful."

(434) The Harry Potter books take place in the 1990s.

(435) In Quidditch, no substitution of players is allowed throughout the game, even if a player is too injured or tired to continue to play.

(436) Diggory is the name of the professor in The Lion, the Witch, and the Wardrobe who travelled to Narnia.

(437) Owls are an important means of communication between wizards in the world of Harry Potter.

(438) When they made Goblet of Fire into a film, digital effects were used in post-production to cover up some of the acne the teen cast members were suffering from.

(439) Natalie McDonald in Harry Potter and Goblet of Fire was inspired by a real girl JK Rowling knew who was dying of

leukemia.

(440) Some fans felt that Hermione's Cinderella moment at the ball in Goblet of Fire didn't really work in the films because Hermione is quite plain in the books whereas Emma Watson looks more like a catalogue model!

(441) One of the reasons why the Harry Potter books have been accused (though never proven) of plagiarism a few times is that magic has been a staple of fiction for as long as books have existed. It is almost impossible to write a book with themes of magic and be 100% original!

(442) The tallest of the Hogwarts towers is the astronomy tower.

(443) Harry Potter and JK Rowling share the same birthday - July the 31st.

(444) Daniel Radcliffe's favourite book in the series is Harry Potter and the Chamber of Secrets.

(445) Harry saving Cedric's body was inspired by the actions of Hector, Achilles, and Patroclus in the Iliad (an ancient Greek poem).

(446) You can buy a Harry Potter Wizard Chess Set created by the Noble Collection. The blurb is - 'Bring the Wizarding World home to your family room with the officially licensed Harry Potter Wizard Chess Set. Go head-to-head in the ultimate duel with this highly detailed miniature recreation of the Wizard Chess Set as seen in Harry Potter and the Sorcerer's Stone. Includes 32 chess pieces, playing board, and two drawstring pouches.'

(447) There is an intricate amount of foreshadowing in the Harry Potter books. The destiny of characters is hinted at early

if you look for clues.

(448) Jude Law was considered for the part of Gilderoy Lockhart but it was felt he looked too young.

(449) Shirley Henderson, the actress who played ghostly student Moaning Myrtle, was actually 37 years-old in real life when she was cast.

(450) You can buy a Harry Potter Magical Beasts Board Game. The blurb goes like this - 'Calling all Wizards! Magical beasts have broken loose at Hogwarts. It's up to you to collect clues to track down the creatures inside and outside of Hogwarts. Watch out though, moving between Hogwarts and the grounds can be treacherous and cost you valuable time. Be the first to collect all the clues and figure out which magical beast you have captured!'

(451) In Quidditch, players may take their wands onto the pitch, but they must not be used on or against any players, any players' broomsticks, the referee, any of the four balls, or the spectators.

(452) A House-elf can live to be around 200 years-old.

(453) Rupert Grint said that he and Emma Watson had casts and moulds made of their buttocks so that the broomstick seats in the films were the right size for them and more comfortable to sit on.

(454) Quidditch is also known as Ikarosfairke or Ikarus ball, which references to the Greek myth of Icarus. In Greek Mythology, Icarus was the Son of Daedalus who dared to fly too near the sun on wings of feathers and wax.

(455) There are 700 different fouls in Quidditch.

(456) The studio wanted The Goblet of Fire to be made into two separate films but the director Mike Newell insisted he could convey the story in one film.

(457) JK Rowling considered the name Draco Spinks before settling on Draco Malfoy. Somehow, Draco Spinks doesn't sound right!

(458) The shortest film in the franchise is Harry Potter and the Deathly Hallows: Part 2.

(459) Emma Watson says her favourite book in the series is Harry Potter and the Prisoner of Azkaban.

(460) Arthur Weasley eventually mended Sirius Black's motorcycle and gifted it to Harry.

(461) Harry Potter and the Prisoner of Azkaban was the last of the films to be released on VHS.

(462) JK Rowling says her favourite author is Jane Austen.

(463) Toadwax and Mugwort are real plants and were found in Culpeper's Complete Herbal.

(464) JK Rowling says that - "I absolutely did not start writing these books to encourage any child into witchcraft. ... I'm laughing slightly because to me, the idea is absurd.

I have met thousands of children now, and not even one time has a child come up to me and said, "Ms. Rowling, I'm so glad I've read these books because now I want to be a witch." They see it for what it is... It is a fantasy world and they understand that completely."

(465) The exterior scenes of Malfoy Manor in The Deathy Hallows were shot at Hardwick Hall.

(466) Platform 7½ leads to the Orient Express.

(467) Katie Leung (Cho) was so nervous about her kissing scene in Order of Phoenix that she couldn't sleep.

(468) Regarding fame, JK Rowling says - "The fame thing is interesting because I never wanted to be famous, and I never dreamt I would be famous. I imagined being a famous writer would be like being like Jane Austen. Being able to sit at home in the parsonage and your books would be very famous and occasionally you would correspond with the Prince of Wales's secretary. You know I didn't think they'd rake through my bins, I didn't expect to be photographed on the beach through long lenses. I never dreamt it would impact my daughter's life negatively, which at times it has."

(469) Daniel Radcliffe said he was very nervous reading the later books because he was fearful that one of the 'golden trio' would be killed off.

(470) JK Rowling wrote a guide for the films to teach the actors how to speak Parseltongue.

(471) Matthew Lewis took home Neville's fake teeth as a memento from his time on the films.

(472) Jason Issacs was so fond of Draco's cane prop that he tried to sneak it off the set and take it home.

(473) Seven is a very magic number in Harry Potter. There are, for example, seven snakes on the door of the Chamber of Secrets.

(474) Rhys Ifans, who played Mr Lovegood in the film series, admitted that he'd never read any of the books before.

(475) Frank Oz, who directed films like The Dark Crystal and Dirty Rotten Scoundrels (but is best known as the voice of Yoda in Star Wars), claims that he turned down an offer to direct Harry Potter and the Chamber of Secrets.

(476) Five 32-ton trucks' worth of polystyrene were needed to produce all the fake rubble for the film version of Deathly Hallows.

(477) If you ever want to play the old Harry Potter And The Sorceror's Stone game on PS here are some handy tips - Collect the chocolate frogs to get energy, Drink and mix the potions to boost energy, Check every bookcase for secret passageways, When flying after the golden snitch you don't have to go through every hoop to be able to grab it, Cast your spell at Voldemort when he is next to the pillars as these topple down on top of him, When rushing to lessons try to get all the beans in those rooms within the time period, When playing chess note that all pieces move directly towards you, When rescuing the kitten make sure it follows you, Pick up any fallen objects for bonus gains in house points.

(478) Six different actors have played Voldemort in the films.

(479) BBC News reported in 2008 that JK Rowling made £5 every second as a result of her book sales.

(480) The Deathy Hallows clocked in at five and a half hours after it was edited for the first time. No wonder it was split up into two films!

(481) The inspiration for Hagrid was a big hells Angels biker who sat next to JK Rowling at a pub when she was nineteen. The biker, despite his intimidating appearance, began talking about his garden and flowers.

(482) Technology is not allowed at Hogwarts because the aura

created by magic works against it. This explains why no one has a television!

(483) Daniel Radcliffe didn't think he would be in all eight films. He thought that an older actor would be cast later on and that he was simply playing Harry as a child.

(484) Maggie Smith battled cancer while shooting the later films. She said "the show must go on" and managed to complete her scenes.

(485) 210,000 coins were made for the scene inside the vault at Gringotts for The Deathly Hallows.

(486) When JK Rowling took the Sorting Hat quiz, she ended up in Hufflepuff.

(487) The day that The Deathly Hallows was published, Emma Watson was in an airport and joined a queue of people waiting to buy a copy. When the other customers deduced who she was they let her go to the front of the line.

(488) Any muggle who stumbles across the site of Hogwarts will see only ruins and not know it's there.

(489) Pumpkin Pasties feature in Harry Potter. A pasty is a baked pastry (it traditionally contains meat and vegetables as the filling) that originated in Cornwall.

(490) The films give one the sense that Beauxbatons is an all-girls school while Durmstrang is an all-boys school. This is not the case with the books.

(491) Emma Watson says that she is addicted to Nutella chocolate spread.

(492) To stop Harry Potter and the Deathly Hollows from a

leak prior to publishing, it was given the secret names Edinburgh Potmakers and The Life and Times of Clara Rose Lovett: An Epic Novel Covering Many Generations.

(493) The spectacles that Daniel Radcliffe wore in the films often had no lenses in them.

(494) When Dumbledore encounters a boggart, he sees the image of his sister Ariana.

(495) One of the older Harry Potter board games is the Harry Potter Diagon Alley Board Game. The blurb is as follows - 'Hurry and visit all the shops of fascinating Diagon Alley to buy wizard school supplies before they run out. The Harry Potter Diagon Alley board game is an exciting race of spending, scheming and casting spells to beat out your opponents. In the world of Harry Potter, Diagon Alley is the long, cobbled street filled with the most amazing shops in the world, accessible only through the Leaky Cauldron Pub in London. Includes game board, 6 trunk cards, 46 Diagon Alley cards, 36 trunk items, 60 wizard coins, 6 moving hats, die and a closed sign. Imported.' Sadly, because it is rather old and hard to buy new now, this game goes for quite a high price.

(496) Rupert Grint owns an ice-cream truck in real life.

(497) JK Rowling says of the strong influence of British folklore in Harry Potter that - "I've taken horrible liberties with folklore and mythology, but I'm quite unashamed about that, because British folklore and British mythology is a totally strange mythology. You know, we've been invaded by people, we've appropriated their gods, we've taken their mythical creatures, and we've soldered them all together to make, what I would say, is one of the richest folklores in the world, because it's so varied. So I feel no compunction about borrowing from that freely, but adding a few things of my own."

(498) The child extras did real homework while shooting classroom scenes in the Harry Potter films.

(499) JK Rowling says it is impossible to get rid of Peeves. "Peeves is like dry rot. You can try [to] eradicate it. It comes with the building. You're stuck. If you've got Peeves, you're stuck."

(500) Simon Fisher-Becker said he signed a four film contract to play the Fat Friar in the Harry Potter films but they left his performance in the first movie on the cutting room floor and never asked him back.

(501) When Tom Felton first met Gary Oldman on the set of Prisoner of Azkaban he thought Oldman was the janitor!

(502) Hagrid is 8'6 tall in the films.

(503) Appare Vestigium is a spell that reveals traces of other recent spells.

(504) Robbie Coltrane said that when he first spoke to JK Rowling about playing Hagrid, she spent four hours on the phone to him explaining the character! This is what convinced him to take the part.

(505) Incarcerous is the fire-making spell.

(506) Tom Felton says that it felt like working on one giant film rather than a series of individual films when they made the Harry Potter series.

(507) When she was asked if Harry was Voldemort's son, JK Rowling said the person who asked the question had watched too much Stars Wars (where Darth Vader was revealed to be Luke Sywalker's father).

(508) Michael Jackson wanted to do a musical version of Harry Potter for the stage but JK Rowling wasn't interested in this idea.

(509) London City Hall, the headquarters of the Greater London Authority, features in the film version of Half-Blood Prince. The hall was only built in 2002 though and so could be classed as an anachronism in the film.

(510) Of Kings Cross Station, JK Rowling wrote - 'It is said (though where the story originated I could not tell you; it is suspiciously vague) that King's Cross station was built either on the site of Boudicca's last battle (Boudicca was an ancient British queen who led a rebellion against the Romans) or on the site of her tomb. Legend has it that her grave is situated somewhere in the region of platforms eight to ten. I did not know this when I gave the wizards' platform its number. King's Cross station takes its name from a now-demolished monument to King George IV. There is a real trolley stuck halfway out of a wall in King's Cross now, and it makes me beam proudly every time I pass...'

(511) Rupert Grint says he considered leaving the film franchise a couple of times. "There were definitely times when I thought about leaving. Filming Harry Potter was a massive sacrifice; working from such a young age for such long periods and I definitely remember thinking during one extended break, 'This whole thing is so all consuming, do I really want to go back? Maybe it's just not for me.' I guess I was probably just being a teenager."

(512) JK Rowling says that Hermione is pretty close to what she was like at that age. "Hermione is me, near enough. A caricature of me when I was younger. I wasn't that clever. But I was that annoying on occasion."

(513) Michael Gambon says that playing a "nice old man" like Dumbledore made a change because he'd played so many crooks and killers in the past.

(514) Guillermo del Toro was asked if he would direct Harry Potter and the Prisoner of Azkaban but he was unavailable because of his commitment to Hellboy.

(515) Daniel Radcliffe said he only became really aware of how big Harry Potter was when he was mobbed in Japan.

(516) Goathland Train Station was used for Hogsmeade Station in the films. Goathland railway station is a station on the North Yorkshire Moors Railway and serves the village of Goathland in the North York Moors National Park, North Yorkshire.

(517) Emma Watson said of her kissing scenes with Rupert Grint and Daniel Radcliffe - "That was awkward. We'd just been soaked by an enormous bucket of water which hurt, which we had to pretend we didn't know was going to drench us but we knew was coming. So, that was equally awkward and weird so both strange situations to be in. Both were complete gentlemen but, you know, it's hard to put our personal history to one side considering we grew up together but I hope they don't mind me saying that once you've done it four or five times kissing gets quite boring, between you and me, so it definitely gets easier."

(518) Mrs Weasley is fond of making Christmas cake. In England, Christmas cake is a fruitcake made with moist currants, sultanas and raisins which have been soaked in rum. The cake usually has white icing. Scotland and other countries around the world have their own variations on the cake.

(519) Ashridge Wood was used in Harry Potter and the Goblet of Fire as the woods for the Quidditch World Cup. Ashridge

Wood is a 39-acre biological Site of Special Scientific in Berkshire. It is in the North Wessex Downs, which is an Area of Outstanding Natural Beauty.

(520) The Glenfinnan Viaduct was used as the bridge to Hogwarts for the Hogarts Express. The bridge is 380 metres long and 31 metres high. It was built in 1898.

(521) Michael Gambon says that the costume department wouldn't let him remove Dumbledore's beard for lunch so it made it very difficult to eat anything!

(522) Nox means night.

(523) During Harry and Hermione's kissing scene in Harry Potter and the Deathly Hallows Part 1, Rupert Grint was banished from the set for laughing.

(524) The Duffer Brothers say that the Mind Flayer in Stranger Things is sort of based on Voldemort in Harry Potter (in that the villain is somewhat unfathomable).

(525) Rupert Grint said he felt a bit lost for a time when the film series ended. He didn't quite know what to do with himself.

(526) Ascendio is a spell that moves objects upwards.

(527) Regarding the lack of Oscar recognition for the Harry Potter series, Emma Watson said - "Well, these books are just so loved, the fans of these books were the most discerning critics and the fact that they've really embraced the series that we made and there are pretty much no complaints – everyone seems to love [them] and think they're true to that. I just don't think there's any better reward than that, than that we've satisfied them."

(528) Emma Watson says she hated Hermione's bushy hair in the early films.

(529) Actors who were considered for the part of Dumbledore after Richard Harris died included Christopher Lee and Peter O'Toole.

(530) Tom Felton said he would love to play James Bond.

(531) Mrs Weasley makes nut brittle in the books. This is hard sugar candy embedded with nuts. Many countries around the world have a tradition of making nut brittle.

(532) Robbie Coltrane says that he loved playing a character like Hagrid who was thoroughly decent and good. "The great thing about Hagrid was that he was a thoroughly good man. It was the first time in my entire career I've played a thoroughly good man. I've played gangsters and prostitutes, transvestites, murderers, everything you can imagine but it's the first time I've played a man who was thoroughly good – and I played it for 10 years… a character that young people could totally trust in."

(533) Colloportus is the door locking spell.

(534) Chris Columbus said that one of the things he loved most about making the first two Harry Potter films is that he was working with a lot of children who were very polite and just grateful to be there.

(535) Bruce Springsteen recorded a song for the first film but it wasn't used because the producers didn't think it meshed with the tone of Harry Potter.

(536) Furnunculus is a charm which will induce boils on your target.

(537) JK Rowling says that brooms are not magical. Magic is directed through them.

(538) Rupert Grint says he enjoyed the Harry Potter experience more on the early films than the later ones. "For the first few Harry Potter films I was living the dream. The reason I auditioned was because I loved the books. When I got to film three or four, I started to feel an overwhelming weight of responsibility because they were so phenomenally popular. The whole press and red carpet thing was an attack on the senses. I don't excel in that kind of environment."

(539) JK Rowling's original Harry Potter pitch to publishers went like this - 'Harry Potter lives with his aunt, uncle and cousin because his parents died in a car-crash — or so he has been told. The Dursleys don't like Harry asking questions; in fact, they don't seem to like anything about him, especially the very odd things that keep happening around him (which Harry himself can't explain). The Dursleys' greatest fear is that Harry will discover the truth about himself, so when letters start arriving for him near his 11th birthday, he isn't allowed to read them. However, the Dursleys aren't dealing with an ordinary postman, and at midnight on Harry's birthday the gigantic Rubeus Hagrid breaks down the door to make sure Harry gets to read his post at last. Ignoring the horrified Dursleys, Hagrid informs Harry that he is a wizard, and the letter he gives Harry explains that he is expected at Hogwarts School of Witchcraft and Wizardry in a month's time. To the Dursleys' fury, Hagrid also reveals the truth about Harry's past. Harry did not receive the scar on his forehead in a car-crash; it is really the mark of the great dark sorcerer Voldemort, who killed Harry's mother and father but mysteriously couldn't kill him, even though he was a baby at the time. Harry is famous among the witches and wizards who live in secret all over the country because Harry's miraculous survival marked Voldemort's downfall. So Harry, who has never had friends or family worth the name, sets off

for a new life in the wizarding world. He takes a trip to London with Hagrid to buy his Hogwarts equipment (robes, wand, cauldron, beginners' draft and potion kit) and shortly afterwards, sets off for Hogwarts from Kings Cross Station (platform nine and three quarters) to follow in his parents' footsteps. Harry makes friends with Ronald Weasley (sixth in his family to go to Hogwarts and tired of having to use second-hand spellbooks) and Hermione Granger (cleverest girl in the year and the only person in the class to know all the uses of dragon's blood). Together, they have their first lessons in magic — astronomy up on the tallest tower at two in the morning, herbology out in the greenhouses where the...'

(540) Tom Felton says that the film series ending wasn't too bad an experience for him. He said it was exciting to go out and do some new things.

(541) Regarding the wide appeal of Harry Potter, David Heyman said - "I think one of the reasons why Harry Potter works is that it's culturally specific but it's thematically universal. It's really about the things that... it's about love and death and loss and friendship and loyalty and good versus evil. We all know characters like Harry, Ron and Hermione, we've all had teachers like Dumbledore and Snape and Lupin – and haven't known too many Voldemorts I hope – but these are people who are... yes, they're British but they are relatable to people all over the world and I think one of the things we can do is find stories that have that universality because we have, when you look – Narnia and Lord of the Rings being the obvious ones – in this country generated and written novels and plays and television series and films that have been seen the world over."

(542) Evanesco is the vanishing spell.

(543) The director Mike Newell says he got a bit carried away at one point with his direction on Goblet of Fire. "When Oliver

and James Phelps, who play Ron's elder twin brothers, Fred and George Weasley, take ageing position ion an attempt to fool the Goblet into believing they're old enough to enter the Tournament, their plan backfired, temporarily rendering them wizened old men. The script called for the twins to blame each other and hit the floor fighting. But I wasn't satisfied with the Phelps' intensity in early takes, so I demanded, "Which one of you wants to fight me" Oliver volunteered, and before he knew it, I wrestled him to the floor. I hadn't planned to demonstrate wrestling, but it just seemed to be a good opportunity to make everyone laugh, even though I pulled a muscle and it hurt like hell for months afterwards! But it's good sometimes to make a complete fool of yourself in front of people who see you as an authority figure. I can't know everything and you don't get the best out of people when they think you do."

(544) Alfonso Cuarón said he had never read any of the books or seen any of the films when he was asked to direct Harry Potter and the Prisoner of Azkaban.

(545) Eleanor Columbus, the daughter of Chris Columbus, is in the first two films as Hogwarts pupil Susan Bones. She doesn't have any dialogue though.

(546) Obliviate is a charm that erases memories.

(547) Emma Watson said - "What does Hermione mean to me? Well, what doesn't she mean to me? She's been like a sister or someone I really know and when people ask what I'll miss the most, of course I will miss the people, but I will actually miss just being her. Coming to work every day and be this girl that lives in this magical world and gets to go on the adventures that she goes on, that's quite devastating."

(548) Rik Mayall, who had his role as Peeves axed from the first film, later said he thought the first Harry Potter movie

was terrible.

(549) Tim Roth passed on the role of Professor Severus Snape to play General Thade in Tim Burton's Planet of the Apes. With the gift of hindsight, that seems like a very bad decision!

(550) JK Rowling said she had to be careful writing about the nature of evil in Harry Potter because these are books for children. "I consciously wanted the first book to be fairly gentle-Harry is very protected when he enters the world. From the publication of Sorcerer's Stone, I've had parents saying to me, My six-year-old loves it, and I've always had qualms about saying, Oh, that's great, because I've always known what's coming. So I have never said these are books for very young children. If you're choosing to write about evil, you really do have a moral obligation to show what that means. So you know what happened at the end of Book IV. I do think it's shocking, but it had to be. It is not a gratuitous act on my part. We really are talking about someone who is incredibly power hungry. Racist, really. And what do those kinds of people do? They treat human life so lightly. I wanted to be accurate in that sense. My editor was shocked by the way the character was killed, which was very dismissive. That was entirely deliberate. That is how people die in those situations. It was just like, You're in my way and you're going to die. It's the first time I cried during the writing of a book, because I didn't want to kill him. "

(551) Humbugs are mentioned in the Harry Potter books. This is a traditional British hard-boiled sweet (candy). They are usually black with white stripes and taste of peppermint.

(552) The scenes at Hagrid's Hut in the first film were shot on a patch of land near Leavesden Studios. The hut was demolished afterwards because they didn't want that patch of land to be hounded by Harry Potter tourists.

(553) Because he'd never read the books, it came as a great shock to Michael Gambon when he learned that Dumbledore was going to die!

(554) Fumos is a handy spell. It creates a bank of smoke and mist.

(555) JK Rowling says that Hagrid was always safe and that she never dreamed of killing him off.

(556) Rupert Grint owns a hovercraft.

(557) Regarding the darkness in the Harry Potter books, JK Rowling says that in her "the cruel artist is stronger than the warm, fuzzy person."

(558) Harry Potter director David Yates says that JK Rowling was never too intrusive in the process of making the films. "Jo Rowling is an incredible partner in these films but she keeps a discreet distance ultimately. She signs off on the screenplay and if she has any issues she communicates them and lets us know what she's happy with and what she's not happy with. And then she's there at the end of the telephone if we need her, basically, and then she'll watch the movie when it's finished. It's the perfect relationship for a group of filmmakers because she's very enthusiastic about what we do, she always supports it, she's not very territorial about her world in the sense that we take some liberties, we trim things out, we add things, and she always supports that. She understands the complexities of adaptation. So, it's a fantastic relationship."

(559) The real Hogwarts Express in the film series is a Hall class steam engine which once belonged to the Great Western Railway.

(560) On why Harry doesn't use the mirror which Sirius has given to contact his godfather in Order of the Phoenix, JK

Rowling says - "Why doesn't he use the mirror? Yeah, I've had that one a lot. Well, as you may have suspected, the mirror is not gone. The mirror is important. The mirror's coming back. A lot of people felt frustrated about that, and I wanted to say that, um, people expect me to tie everything up neatly. But life isn't like that. And I felt that Harry made this strong decision which he shouldn't have gone back on. I'm not going to use this mirror, I will never use this mirror, I'm not going to lure Sirius out of hiding. That's the mirror gone into my case, I'm forgetting about the mirror. Then he panics, when he thinks that Sirius is being tortured and yes, he's forgotten about the mirror. I needed him to forget about the mirror plot-wise. I wanted him to have the mirror, I didn't want him to use the mirror, so my excuse for that is, um, you know, that he made the resolution and then forgets, in his panic. I think that holds up. But I accept that a lot of people found that unsatisfying, and there may have been other ways to do that. Although I couldn't think of another way, and I did try."

(561) Aqua Eructo is a spell that makes water shoot from the wand.

(562) Emma Watson says she loves to bake in her spare time and is famed for her chocolate chip banana bread.

(563) Fred and George Weasley were born on April Fools Day.

(564) Rooms in the Department of Mysteries The Brain Room are The Death Chamber, containing the Veil, The Hall of Prophecy, The Locked Room, containing "Love", The Planet Room, The Time Room.

(565) When asked what she would change about the books, JK Rowling said - "There are bits of all six books that I would go back and tighten up. My feeling is that Phoenix is overlong, but I challenge anyone to find the obvious place to cut. There are places that I would prune, now, looking back, but they

wouldn't add up to a hugely reduced book, because my feeling is you need what's in there. You need what's in there if I'm going to play fair for the reader in the resolution in Book 7. One of the reasons Phoenix is so long is that I had to move Harry around a lot, physically. There were places he had to go he had never been before, and that took time to get him there, to get him away. That was the longest non-Hogwarts stretch in any of the books, and that's really what bumps up the length. I'm trying to think of specifics, it's hard."

(566) Ludo Bagman is Head of the Department of Magical Games and Sports in the Ministry of Magic. 'Ludo' means 'I play'.

(567) The home of Sirius Black in Order of the Phoenix used the same set that depicted the home of Robert Downey Jr as Sherlock Holmes in a 2009 film.

(568) Jason Isaacs said that he didn't like it when people called the Harry Potter films a franchise. "It always upsets me when I hear it called a franchise because that's when someone sells burgers and someone says I'll have some of that and opens a shop selling burgers as well. This is one story, essentially, that has taken 10 years to tell so beautifully, and with such care, it seems to me there isn't one drop of cynicism in anyone's participation, or mine."

(569) Lumos Maxim is a spell that summons forth a beam of light. Handy if trapped in a cave!

(570) One of the flying cars in the Chamber of Secrets film was stolen by thieves.

(571) Hatty Jones, star of the enjoyable 1998 children's film Madeline, tested for the part of Hermione.

(572) JK Rowling says that evil can sometimes seem attractive.

"Yes, I think that's very true. Harry has seen the kind of people who are grouped around this very evil character. I think we'd all acknowledge that the bully in the playground is attractive. Because if you can be his friend, you are safe. This is just a pattern. Weaker people, I feel, want that reflected glory. I'm trying to explore that. It's great to hear feedback from the kids."

(573) The bats in Hagrid's hut in Harry Potter and the Prisoner of Azkaban were real.

(574) The Weasley twins in the films are not redheads in real life.

(575) JK Rowling says that fans were always more concerned about her killing Ron than Hermione. "Mostly they are really worried about Ron. As if I'm going to kill Harry's best friend. What I find interesting is only once has anyone said to me - Don't kill Hermione, and that was after a reading when I said no one's ever worried about her. Another kid said - Yeah, well, she's bound to get through OK. They see her as someone who is not vulnerable, but I see her as someone who does have quite a lot of vulnerability in her personality."

(576) Rupert Grint says it was hard to adjust to life after Harry Potter. "The line between Ron and me became thinner with each film and I think we became virtually the same person. There's a lot of me in Ron and moving on was a massive adjustment because it was such a constant part of my life. I don't want to liken it to coming out of prison because it wasn't a prison, but it did feel like stepping out of an institution. It was nice to breathe the fresh air and now I'm really enjoying stepping further away from that blue-screen world."

(577) Most members of the Black family take their names from stars.

(578) Accio means 'I summon'.

(579) Emma Watson says she felt guilty growing up for not enjoying fame very much. She felt it was all wasted on her.

(580) Richard Harris had trouble remembering his lines when he played Dumbledore so he and Daniel Radcliffe would privately run through their scenes together to help each other.

(581) Harry Potter and the Prisoner of Azkaban is the lowest grossing of the Potter films (yet some might say it was the best film).

(582) Michael Gambon says he was never given any specific instructions on how to approach playing Dumbledore after the death of Richard Harris. "No one ever spoke to me about it. Not a word. On the first film I did, which was directed by Alfonso Cuaron, I walked in there and I'm naturally Irish and my first accent is Irish, I will speak Irish with my parents, and I played just a slight touch of Trinity College Dublin. That light lilt. And no one's ever mentioned it."

(583) Bouillabaisse is mentioned in the Harry Potter books. This is a French fish stew.

(584) JK Rowling thinks that younger kids can be surprisingly resilient when it comes to scary stuff in books. "In some ways, I think younger children tend to be more resilient. It's kids who are slightly older who really get the scariness of it. Possibly because they have come across more intense stuff in their own lives."

(585) At the Orlando Harry Potter resort you can buy Butterbeer ice-cream. They also serve ice-cream in these flavours - Banana, Chocolate, Granny Smith, Mint, Pistachio, Vanilla, Orange Marmalade, Toffee, Toffee Apple, Strawberries & Cream, Chocolate Chili, Apple Crumble,

Vanilla, Salted Caramel Blondie, Clotted Cream, Earl Grey & Lavender, Sticky Toffee Pudding, Chocolate & Raspberry, Strawberry & Peanut Butter.

(586) Tilda Swinton turned down the part of Professor Trelawney. Swinton said she didn't like Harry Potter because it (in her view) romanticised boarding-schools.

(587) Tom Felton says that "dying my hair blonde was slightly arduous after 10 years. Even though it seemed to build some sort of super-human resistance, it still seems to be OK, so I'm not suffering too badly. But that got slightly painful after six or seven years."

(588) The only Hogwarts sets built for the first film were the Great Hall, the Grand Staircase, and the Gryffindor Common Room.

(589) Signed copies of The Goblet of Fire first edition with JK Rowling's signature can now change hands for more than $10,000.

(590) Silvanus Kettleburn is a Hogwarts Care of Magical Creatures professor. 'Silva' means woodland.

(591) Harry Potter's name could refer to a potter's field. Potter's field is of Biblical origin, referring to Akeldama (meaning field of blood in Aramaic), stated to have been purchased, with the coins that had been paid to Judas Iscariot for his identification of Jesus, after Judas' suicide, by the high priests of Jerusalem. A potter's field, paupers' grave or common grave is a place for the burial of unknown, unclaimed or indigent people.

(592) Chris Columbus was back in the world of YA film adaptations when he directed Percy Jackson & the Olympians: The Lightning Thief in 2010. This was based on the books by

Rick Riordan. The film got mixed reviews though and didn't turn into a franchise.

(593) Finite Incantatum is a spell that stops other spells.

(594) The first Deathly Hallows is the only movie not to feature Dame Maggie Smith as Professor Minerva McGonagall.

(595) Rupert Grint once said he has never watched any of the Harry Potter movies again since attending their premieres. "It's just something I've never really wanted to watch. Not that it's kind of cringey or anything, but I mean ... it was us growing up. It kind of documents our lives. And the most awkward stages of being a teenager, and so it's a weird thing. It's a weird perspective watching them."

(596) In a later interview though, Grint said he had watched the first film again recently and found it a pleasant and "therapeutic" experience.

(597) Malham Cove was used in Harry Potter and the Deathly Hallows Part 1. Malham Cove is a natural limestone rock formation near the village of Malham.

(598) Voldemort embracing Draco was improvised by Ralph Fiennes for the Deathly Hallows. This explains Tom Felton's believably confused reaction.

(599) Patrick McGoohan was considered for the part of Dumbledore in the first film. McGoohan is best known as Number Six in the brilliant 1960s mystery/spy series The Prisoner. McGoohan was in poor health though at the time and so not a viable option even if he had been interested.

(600) On directing the last film in the series, David Yates said - "For the very last shot, Dan, Rupert and Emma had to run and

jump and throw themselves on to this giant blue mat. I thought that'd be a really appropriate way to end it: a leap into the wide blue yonder. After I yelled Cut, Dan gave a speech. So did David Heyman and I. It was very emotional."

(601) Azkaban was a fortress rather than a prison and never appeared on muggle or wizard maps.

(602) ABeBooks say that, when it comes to rare or valuable editions of the first book that - 'Hardcover first edition first printings of Harry Potter and the Philosopher's Stone have become the 'Holy Grail' for Potter collectors. If you find one in the attic, then you've hit the jackpot. Only 500 were published and 300 went to libraries. The main characteristics of a 1997 first edition first printing are a print line that reads "10 9 8 7 6 5 4 3 2 1" and the crediting of "Joanne Rowling" not J.K. Prices on AbeBooks vary from £28,850 to £39,700. A handful of advance proof copies are available from £5,400 to £9,700. Prices for Australian first editions vary between £145 and £1,445. The first editions of the deluxe edition from 1999 are also desirable with prices from £320 to £1,800. Paperback first editions of the Philosopher's Stone are also quite scarce and attract four-figure price-tags - sometimes five figures if in excellent condition.'

(603) Harry worked as an Auror before becoming the Herbology Professor at Hogwarts.

(604) Ralph Fiennes said he got into character as Voldemort by picturing him as lonely. "Young Voldemort was an orphan and denied any kind of parental affection or love, so he's been an isolated figure from a very young age. But I always think there has to be the possibility of good in someone, too. It might have been eroded, repressed, suppressed or somehow distorted within him after he was really damaged."

(605) Notice how the pink outfits of Dolores Umbridge in the

Order of the Phoenix film get darker and darker to express her mood.

(606) Harry Potter and the Chamber of Secrets has the lowest rating of the Potter films on IMDB.

(607) The highest rated of the Potter films on IMDB is Harry Potter and the Deathly Hallows: Part 2.

(608) Rupert Grint said in an interview once that he had no idea what to do with the personal wealth (estimated to be $50 million) that the Harry Potter series had afforded him. Apart from purchase hovercrafts and ice-cream vans we presume!

(609) David Heyman said of the books that "I hadn't a clue the Potter books would become an international phenomenon but I loved the author's voice, that the book didn't talk down to kids and it made me laugh."

(610) The Sloth Grip Roll is a Quidditch move where a player dodges a Bludger by hanging upside-down from his or her broom.

(611) Professor Dumbledore likes sherbet lemons because JK Rowling loves them too.

(612) Virginia Water was used to represent Hogwarts' lake where Harry rode on the Hippogriff in the Prisoner of Azkaban. Virginia Water is a village in northern Surrey, home to the Wentworth Estate and the Wentworth Club. This beautiful area has some of the most expensive property prices in Britain and many celebrities have lived there.

(613) The Seven Sisters cliffs were used in the film version of Goblet of Fire. The Seven Sisters are a series of chalk cliffs by the English Channel. They form part of the South Downs in East Sussex, between the towns of Seaford and Eastbourne.

(614) In the first book, Harry doesn't utter a word until the second chapter.

(615) Terry Gilliam said that Warner Bros approached him about directing one of the later Harry Potter films but, still smarting from not getting the first movie, he turned them down.

(616) In total, all seven Harry Potter books contain 1,084,170 words.

(617) Those 1,084,170 words that make up the Potter books take up 6,095 pages!

(618) JK Rowling seriously thought about Draco Smart as a name before she settled on Malfoy.

(619) Claremont Square is the exterior of Grimmauld Place in the film version of Order of the Phoenix. Claremont Square is in Islington - a London Borough. The shape of Claremont Square is unusual because in the 18th century a water reservoir was on that land. The houses have a steep incline.

(620) Voldemort was born on New Year's Eve 1926.

(621) When the Harry Potter films ended, Daniel Radcliffe said that he hoped to work with Rupert Grint and Emma Watson again one day. At the time of writing this has yet to happen.

(622) The scene in the first Deathly Hallows where Hermione and Harry dance was not in the books and was only written for the film.

(623) Chris Columbus lobbied for the director's chair on the first film because his children loved the books.

(624) When Harry is taught how to use his wand by Professor Flitwick in Chamber of secrets, this scene was shot in a classroom at Harrow School in Harrow on the Hill.

(625) Visual effects supervisor Tim Alexander says that the Inferius attack in Half-Blood Prince was very difficult to do and took several months.

(626) The fantastical sweets and chocolate in the world of Harry Potter obviously owe a big debt to Charlie and the Chocolate Factory.

(627) It is said that if all the Harry Potter books ever sold were laid end to end they would stretch around the world more than a dozen times!

(628) JK Rowling says she was surprised (and perhaps a little disappointed) that her young daughter didn't find the end of Goblet of Fire upsetting!

(629) Jamie Campbell Bower auditioned for the role of young Tom Riddle but missed out. He did though land the part of a young Grindelwald in Deathly Hallows Part 1.

(630) French actress Carole Bouquet was wanted for the part of Madame Maxime but she couldn't get out of a contract with Studio Canal. The part went to Frances de la Tour instead.

(631) Auror means a Professional Dark-wizard catcher.

(632) Legilimency is the magic ability to extract thoughts from another person. A mind reading ability.

(633) David Heyman said that he was wasn't sure if they would manage to adapt all seven books into films. That was obviously dependent on whether they were financially

successful enough at the box-office to keep making them. He said that after the fourth film he was finally confident that they would be able to adapt all of them.

(634) The reason why Prisoner of Azkaban felt like a cinematic departure for the film series is that Alfonso Cuarón has his own distinctive style and loves hand-held camera shots.

(635) The first Deathly Hallows film was going to be released in 3D but this plan was scrapped in the end because they didn't have enough time.

(636) The incantation Avada Kedavra is the Killing Curse - one of the three Unforgivable Curses.

(637) St Pancras Renaissance Hotel was used as the entrance to King's Cross station in Harry Potter and The Chamber of Secrets.

(638) The writer Neil Gaiman dismissed a newspaper claim that JK Rowling had borrowed ideas from one of his books for Harry Potter as "lazy journalism".

(639) Millennium Bridge is in Harry Potter and the Half-Blood Prince. The Millennium Bridge is a steel suspension bridge for pedestrians crossing the River Thames in London, linking Bankside with the City of London. It opened in 2000.

(640) Paul Whitehouse originally had a much more significant role as Sir Cadogan in Goblet of Fire but it was almost completely cut from the film.

(641) A Seeker is a Quidditch player who attempts to catch the Golden Snitch.

(642) The initial Hardback run by Bloomsbury of the first Harry Potter book published only 500 copies.

(643) Helena Bonham Carter consulted Emma Watson for the scene where Hermione takes the Polyjuice Potion to disguise herself as Bellatrix. Emma Watson said it was strange watching someone try to impersonate her because you obviously aren't aware of your own personal mannerisms.

(644) David Thewlis was persuaded to be in Harry Potter by his friend and fellow Harry Potter cast member Ian Hart.

(645) Julie Walters said that if she'd known Mark Williams was going to join the Harry Potter cast she would have used her natural Midlands accent to be in sync with him.

(646) JK Rowling said she experienced a huge sense of relief when the last Harry Potter book was finished.

(647) Custard creams feature in the Harry Potter books. This is a biscuit (cookie) which you will find in any British supermarket.

(648) Hermione seems to like a little ginger in her Butterbeer.

(649) Regarding rare editions of Harry Potter and the Prisoner of Azkaban, AbeBooks say - 'The initial hardcover print run was stopped mid-printing after it was discovered that 'Joanne Rowling' rather than 'J.K. Rowling' had been printed on the copyright page. Joanne versions are available for prices starting at around £1,080 and go up to £8,650 for signed pristine copies. First edition first printings will have the number line "10 9 8 7 6 5 4 3 2 1" and a block of misaligned text on page seven. Opinions about the number of copies printed before the errors were spotted vary greatly - however, it seems that only a small number came off the press which greatly enhances its value. The deluxe editions, with green cloth, of 1999 are also collectible if they are a first edition (prices go up to £3,600). However, second printings can be picked up for

three figures. Look out for Canadian first editions, published by Raincoast, for between £75 and £215. First American editions vary from £110 to £500 for a signed copy.'

(650) If you have a copy of Harry Potter and the Deathly Hallows, AbeBooks say it will only be worth anything if it was signed by JK Rowling. 'Millions and millions of copies of Harry Potter and the Deathly Hallows have been published. J.K. Rowling launched the book at London's Natural History Museum in 2007. She signed copies of the book that night for 1,700 people who won exclusive tickets to the event. Those 1,700 copies have considerable value now. Prices for signed copies usually start around £720. The most expensive signed Hallows to sell via AbeBooks went for £4,000.'

(651) Aparecium is an incantation to reveal hidden writing.

(652) The Dementors were going to be conveyed by practical effects only in the films but this proved too difficult. In the end they were filmed underwater (to create the floating effect) and then enhanced with a little computer animation.

(653) Emma Watson said that she felt a pang of sadness six months after the last Harry Potter film because six months was usually the length of time the actors got off before they went back to make the next film. For the first time in years they would not be going back.

(654) Sir Richard Attenborough was said to have been interested in the part of Dumbledore when Richard Harris passed away.

(655) Lego produced some new Harry Potter sets in 2020. The details are: Hogwarts Room of Requirement - 193 pieces including 3 minifigures: Harry Potter, Hermione Granger and Luna Lovegood, Hogwarts Astronomy Tower - 253 pieces including 3 minifigures: Harry Potter, Hermione Granger and

Dolores Umbridge, Hedwig - 630 pieces, with a wingspan of over 13" and a beak-to-tail measurement of over 7", Privet Drive - 797 pieces including 6 minifigures: Harry Potter, Ron Weasley, Dudley Dursley, Vernon Dursley, Petunia Dursley and Dobby, Forbidden Forest - 971 pieces including 8 minifigures: Harry Potter, Hermione Granger, Horace Slughorn, Luna Lovegood, Neville Longbottom, Ron Weasley, Lavender Brown and Draco Malfoy, Attack on The Burrow - 1,047 pieces including 8 minifigures: Ron, Ginny, Arthur and Molly Weasley, Nymphadora Tonks, Bellatrix Lestrange, Fenrir Greyback and Harry Potter

(656) Marc Forster turned down the chance to direct Prisoner Of Azkaban. Forster directed films like Finding Neverland and Quantum of Solace.

(657) JK Rowling invented Quidditch after an argument with a boyfriend. "I don't really know what the connection is between the row and Quidditch except that Quidditch is quite a violent game and maybe in my deepest, darkest soul I would quite like to see him hit by a bludger."

(658) Daniel Radcliffe said that he and his child co-stars had to get casts of their teeth made for the first film. This was so that a fake tooth could be quickly made if one fell out.

(659) Tanya Seghatchian, the co-producer/executive producer on the films, said - "One of the great pleasures of the series is to look at the first films, then see how far the younger actors have come; it's like Michael Apted's 7 Up, where you feel you've watched these people grow up on screen, and become part of your family. Every director, and all those great actors, have left their mark on them."

(660) Deathly Hallows Part 2 broke the record for the biggest weekend box-office opening. It held the record for only ten months though until the release of Marvel's The Avengers.

(661) One of the reasons why Harry Potter is successful is that eschews the modern world and technology and gives us heroes who have a simpler (if hardly trouble free) way of life where nature, history, and friendship is more important than what brand of phone you have. The world of Harry Potter, with steam trains, castles, myths and legends, midnight feasts, is timeless and anachronistic. A trip to Hogwarts is like going back in time to escape from the present. This is what gives Harry Potter that comfort blanket feel which charmed readers around the world.

(662) Robson Green was considered for the role of Sirius Black.

(663) Sean Connery was apparently one of the people considered for the part of Dumbledore in the first film but was not interested. Connery had already made a big mistake by turning down the part of Gandalf in Lord of the Rings. He said he didn't really understand fantasy scripts.

(664) Trifle features in the Harry Potter books. This is an old English dessert that contains layers of fruit, jelly, custard, sponge, with whipped cream on top.

(665) On 25 May 2014, Emma Watson graduated from Brown University with a bachelor's degree in English literature.

(666) The filmmakers were going to exclude the battle between McGonagall and Snape in the Deathly Hallows but JK Rowling insisted that it must be in the movie.

(667) Basilisk is snake-like creature with a gaze that will turn you to stone. This is like Medusa in Greek mythology. In European bestiaries and legends, a basilisk is a legendary reptile reputed to be a serpent king, who can cause death with a single glance.

(668) One of the reasons why Chris Columbus directed the first Harry Potter film was that he took the time and trouble to write a new draft of the script free of charge. This impressed the studio and illustrated how passionate he was about the project.

(669) Ralph Fiennes says he was quite glad that kids found Voldemort scary. "When I was young, there was this character in Chitty Chitty Bang Bang called the Child Catcher. I remember being terrified by this figure. I think children should be really scared of Lord Voldemort."

(670) Wizengamot is the Wizard High Court and consists of about fifty witches and wizards

(671) The door leading to the Chamber of Secrets in the films was mechanical rather than CGI.

(672) The fact that the Harry Potter film series had four different directors worked to its advantage in the sense that a fresh creative sensibility was injected into the franchise on a regular basis.

(673) The name Snape comes from the village of Snape in Suffolk.

(674) Anna Friel lobbied to play the role of Nymphadora Tonks in the films so she could work with her (then) real-life partner David Thewlis but she didn't get the part.

(675) When Daniel Radcliffe was linked to the part of Bilbo Baggins in The Hobbit film, he was quick to downplay the speculation. "I wouldn't like to get involved with another franchise at all, really. I've done that, and I know what that's like, and it's been a wonderful thing. Going on to any other franchise after Potter might seem a little bit of a letdown. I

don't think I would be asked to play Bilbo. It's a ridiculous rivalry [Harry Potter vs. Lord of the Rings] completely built up by the media, but I certainly would be wary of getting involved in another magical fantasy franchise."

(676) In a 2019 interview, Dame Maggie Smith said - "I am deeply grateful for the work in Potter and indeed Downton Abbey, but it wasn't what you'd call satisfying. I didn't really feel I was acting in those things."

(677) A Secret Keeper is someone with a secret concealed within them using the Fidelius Charm.

(678) Indian filmmaker Mira Nair, best known for Salaam Bombay, turned down an offer to direct Harry Potter and the Order of the Phoenix.

(679) The Disillusionment Charm camouflages a person so that they blend into their surroundings.

(680) Hagrid likes Bath buns in the books. Bath buns are a sweet roll topped with sugar.

(681) Stuart Craig, the production designer on the Potter films, said that it wasn't always easy to be faithful to the books and the continuity of the movies. "The geography and architecture of Hogwarts sometimes didn't fit as we went along because we couldn't have foreseen at the start what was coming. Nobody seemed to mind. Sirius Black was imprisoned in a cell at the top of a tower. A couple of movies later, it was replaced by the astronomy tower from which Dumbledore falls to his death. We took incredible liberties with continuity from one film to another. Everyone has been very tolerant; we seem to be forgiven every time."

(682) Warner Brothers received some very angry complaints when the film of Harry Potter and the Half-Blood Prince was

pushed back to 2009 (it was supposed to be released in 2008).

(683) Lucius Malfoy's line, "Let us hope Mr. Potter will always be around to save the day," was improvised by Jason Isaacs.

(684) Jelly-Legs Jinx is a handy magic jinx that will make your opponent's legs wobble and collapse.

(685) Australia House doubled for Gringotts in the films. Australia House is the home of the Australian High Commission in London.

(686) Harry Potter And The Deathly Hallows features a poster of Equus in a cafe scene. Equus is the name of a play that Daniel Radcliffe starred in.

(687) Rupert Grint said that, regarding fame and growing-up, - "I could feel this growing narrative willing me to get engulfed in some big scandal off-screen. It felt like people were waiting for me to go off the rails, but it was never going to happen. We filmed the whole thing in this very intense bubble in Watford not Hollywood, so we didn't have the chance."

(688) Forty versions of Slytherin's locket were made for the scene in which Harry and Ron try to destroy it in Harry Potter and the Deathly Hallows: Part 1.

(689) Regarding rare or valuable editions of Harry Potter and the Goblet of Fire, AbeBooks say - 'JK's signature (by book 4, she was signing fewer copies) turns any first edition of Goblet of Fire into a book with a four-figure price-tag but there are a handful of copies over £7,200. Look out for the limited editions with original watercolour illustrations by Giles Greenfield (Bloomsbury's UK edition) and Mary GrandPré (Scholastic's super rare US edition of only 25 copies). If either illustrator has signed a copy, then prices are again in four-

figures. Many buyers are also looking for books accompanied by items such as entrance wristbands or golden tickets from events where JK Rowling has conducted a signing. After the Goblet of Fire, these signing events have become increasingly scarce.'

(690) In her early notes for Harry Potter, JK Rowling had different subjects at Hogwarts. These were simply titled Alchemy, Beasts, and Herbalism.

(691) Between the filming of The Chamber of Secrets and The Prisoner of Azkaban, the real-life train used for the Hogwarts Express was damaged by vandals.

(692) Chris Columbus thinks that Daniel Radcliffe will be like Ron Howard. That is to say a well adjusted former child star who enjoys a long and productive career on whatever side of the camera he chooses.

(693) Ray Winstone turned down the part of Mad-Eye Moody in the films. "I nearly did a Potter movie. They earn fortunes from those films but for the time that is involved in making one they don't want to pay you. I'm sorry, but I make movies to get a living. Besides, I would have made two films in the time it would have taken to make one Potter movie."

(694) When Alan Rickman passed away in 2016, JK Rowling said - "There are no words to express how shocked and devastated I am to hear of Alan Rickman's death. He was a magnificent actor and a wonderful man."

(695) Sausages and mash feature in the books. This dish is commonly known as bangers and mash in England.

(696) Ralph Fiennes says he nearly turned down the part of Voldemort because he didn't know anything about Harry Potter. "The truth is I was actually ignorant about the films

and the books. I was approached by the production. Mike Newell was directing the film that they wanted me to be in... the first time Voldemort was going to appear physically. Out of ignorance I just sort of thought, this isn't for me. Quite stupidly I resisted, I was hesitant."

(697) Rhubarb crumble is mentioned in the books. This is an English dessert where fruit is topped with a flour, butter and sugar mix to create a sweet crunchy topping when baked. In America a crumble is known as a crisp.

(698) People struggled to pronounce Hermione correctly so a moment in Goblet of Fire was included where she teaches Viktor Krum to pronounce her name.

(699) Production designer Stuart Craig says that Diagon Alley in the films was designed to be like a twisted version of Dickens. "What we did there was a mix of images seen from the real world — 17th/18th century London and I think we distressed it more. There are examples of the Lanes in Brighton and in the city of York, where the structures are correct, but they're all too smart and done up. We wanted crumbling, ancient dereliction because they kept pace with the antiquity of the place and the fact that these people living in the wizarding world wouldn't care about that, particularly. So it's as full of character as we could possibly make it."

(700) Hypable ranked Prisoner of Azkaban (which they played on PS2) as the best of the Harry Potter video games. 'Far and away the best game in the Harry Potter series in my opinion, effectively creating an open-world-ish model of gameplay while allowing the player to feel like their actions advance the plot.'

(701) Dumbledore's phoenix Fawkes obviously takes his name from Guy Fawkes. Guy Fawkes Day is celebrated in Britain every year on the 5th of November. The day is celebrated to

commemorate the Gunpowder Plot of the year 1605. The (foiled) Gunpowder Plot was meant to kill King James I and destroy Parliament. One of the main conspirators of the plot was Guy Fawkes, after which the day is named. On November the 5th, bonfire parties and fireworks are still common in Britain.

(702) The Harry Potter books were the first children's books to make the New York Times Bestseller list since EB White's Charlotte's Web in 1952.

(703) Hermione is pronounced her-MY-oh-knee.

(704) Ginny's name is short for Ginevra. This is inspired by Guinevere, the queen of Camelot.

(705) A witch or wizard's Pensieve, as with their wand, is buried with them.

(706) Orlando Ticket Deals had this to say about the Fishy Green Ale you can buy at the Wizarding World of Harry Potter - 'We know the name might not sound too appealing, and come to think of it the colour too, but don't let that put you off! If you fancy being a bit adventurous (and want to get some good Instagram snaps while you're at it), then this is the one for you. Fishy Green Ale is a refreshing drink with a creamy consistency and hints of mint and cinnamon. A bed of fish eggs lies at the bottom, but don't worry the only surprise will be bursts of tangy blueberry flavour!'

(707) The Death Eaters have some obvious parallels with the Nazis in Adolf Hitler's Germany.

(708) The Hogwarts motto is Draco domiens nunquan titillandus. Which is Latin for 'Never tickle a sleeping dragon'.

(709) Baubillious is a charm that produces a bright, yellow-

white bolt of lightning from the tip of a wand.

(710) Two alternate titles for the final book were Harry Potter and the Elder Wand and Harry Potter and the Peverell Quest.

(711) JK Rowling says it took at least a year to write a new Harry Potter book.

(712) Costume designer Jany Temime came on board for Harry Potter and the Prisoner of Azkaban and stayed for the rest of the series. She decided to dress the kids in the films more like normal modern teenagers than Victorian boarding school children. "The Prisoner of Azkaban has something very special," she said. "It's the first dark one. I wanted to change things, because I knew that sort of A Christmas Carol aesthetic was not at all the style. It was good for little kids, but a teenager would never go and watch that film, so we wanted to make it cooler. We needed to make the kids look like real next-door kids."

(713) The Harry Potter books reminded some readers of Diana Wynne Jones 1977 book Charmed Life. The book is about two orphans who are taught about magic in a castle. "I think Ms Rowling did get quite a few of her ideas from my books," said Jones, "though I have never met her, so I have never been able to ask her. My books were written many years before the Harry Potter books so any similarities probably come from what she herself read as a child. Once a book is published, out in the world, it is sort of common property, for people to take ideas from and use, and I think this is what happened to my books."

(714) The name Argus Filch has obvious subtexts. Filch means to steal while Argusi an all-seeing monster in Greek mythology.

(715) The inscription on Dumbledore's family tomb ('Where

your treasure is, your heart will be also') is from Matthew 6:21.

(716) According to Ranker, the two things in the films that fans of the books were disappointed by the most was Harry not repairing his wand with the Elder Wand in Deathly Hallows and the movie version of Ginny Weasley (who some fans thought lacked the charisma and spark of Ginny in the books).

(717) JK Rowling says that Harry Potter wasn't based on anyone she knew as a child.

(718) Tom Felton says that after the third Harry Potter film the costume department sewed up the pockets of Draco's robes because of his habit of sneaking, sweets, food, and drink onto the set.

(719) The humble Ford Anglia car got a fresh wave of love when Harry Potter came out. Liam Payne bought one and it was 'modded' into Grand Theft Auto.

(720) The Ford Anglia in the film series was real. It was a 1962 model. JK Rowling says she loved Ford Anglias because her boyfriend had one when she was a student.

(721) Production designer Stuart Craig says that he loves the anachronistic nature of Harry Potter, the strange mix of old and new. "Because they have magic they don't need technology so everything has a vaguely 1950s look about it and I can't claim that was a conscious decision in the beginning but it's implicit in the books. The Hogwarts Express is a steam train and steam trains finished in this country in the early 60s so that sets the feeling of where it is in terms of technology. But it's the most wonderful mix in that they wear jeans and T shirts, use 50s technology, live in 13th, 14th, 15th century surroundings and we are deliberately exploiting those different influences and letting periods clash together in an

energetic dynamic way. "

(722) David Thewlis said - "I love doing the Harry Potter films. It's such a big family, everyone knows each other very well and have worked together for so long on these films. The other good thing is you know it's going to get seen, that it will be in the cinemas. This isn't always the case with films you make. You know millions of people are going to see it. The thing about Harry Potter is it's great fun because of the people – I was usually with Julie Walters and Mark Williams, Brendan Gleeson, Robbie Coltrane and the kids.

Wonderful, funny, amazing people. If you're going to hang around on a set bored, you might as well do it with Julie Walters. It'll never happen again. You'll never have three child actors going through adolescence just working on that one film, which is such a success. It's been seven years in story time, 10 or 11 years in film time. Dan (Daniel Radcliffe] was only ten when he started but he's remained totally sane. Not only sane but lovely and amazing. He's a gorgeous guy, very articulate, very level-headed and funny. He's never anything but really good company. He's grown up into a beautiful young man. I love him."

(723) Bombarda Maxima is the incantation of a charm that produces large explosions.

(724) Costume designer Jany Temime says she took inspiration from Rugby and American Football strips when she designed the Quidditch uniforms for the films.

(725) JK Rowling was awarded the Légion d'honneur in 2009. This is the highest award France can bestow. "I want to thank my French readers for not resenting my choice of a French name (Voldemort) for my evil character," she said at the ceremony. "I can assure you that the decision did not come from any anti-French sentiment but I needed a name that

evoked both power and exoticism."

(726) The Muggle-Repelling Charm is (obviously) a charm used to ward away Muggles.

(727) Fantastic Beasts and Where to Find Them is a 2001 guide book written by JK Rowling under the pen name of the fictitious author Newt Scamander about the magical creatures in the Harry Potter universe. The 128 page book was written to benefit Comic Relief but later became the basis for a new series of spin-off prequels.

(728) JK Rowling said of Fantastic Beasts and Where to Find Them that "this film is neither a prequel, nor a sequel to the Harry Potter series, but an extension of the wizarding world. Newt's story will start in New York City, seventy years before Harry gets underway."

(729) JK Rowling says that the greatest gift she could have would be to think that the Harry Potter books had fostered a love of reading in someone. "The thing I would most like to think I had imparted to anyone is a love of reading. I mean that. If I felt that even one person had grown to a better appreciation or to a love of books, and that had started with Harry, I think I would die happy. That's all I wanted."

(730) Daniel Radcliffe does not have any social media apart from Instagram. "There's a bunch of reasons I'm not on Twitter and stuff, and part of it is that I'm lazy and I wouldn't be able to respond to everyone, it would stress me out."

(731) The Hogwarts Pensieve is composed of carved stone and is engraved with modified Saxon runes.

(732) JK Rowling invented the Houses of Hogwarts on the back of an airplane sick bag!

(733) David Heyman has conceded that Chris Columbus was a very 'conservative' choice to direct the first Harry Potter film.

(734) Incendio Tria is a charm that produces flames.

(735) The film of Fantastic Beasts and Where to Find Them marked JK Rowling's debut as a screenwriter.

(736) In 2000, JK Rowling read to more than 20,000 people at Toronto's Skydome. This set a Guinness World Record for the largest audience at a book reading.

(737) JK Rowling said she was very moved when she went on her first American book tour because it illustrated to her how children around the world loved Harry Potter.

(738) Costume designer Jany Temime says that Daniel, Rupert, and Emma never had any great interest in the costumes they wore in Harry Potter and never offered any opinions. They simply wanted to get on with making the film!

(739) The Verdimillious Charm (Verdimillious) produces green sparks of energy from a wand.

(740) JK Rowling says that if Snape had an odour it would be of "bitterness and old shoes."

(741) A Harry Potter chocolate bar came out around the time of the first film. It was described as Milk chocolate with fizzy sprinkles and a mystery filling. Reviews were mixed with tasters never quite managing to work out what it was supposed to be. Lime, mint, and 'green caramel' was their best guess.

(742) In French, Voldemort means "Flight of Death".

(743) JK Rowling has said that another Mitford sister, Jessica,

was a big inspiration to her. Jessica Mitford, in contrast to some of her siblings, was a communist and civil rights activist. Andromeda in Harry Potter, who is not like her sisters, seems analogous to Jessica Mitford and her sisters. "My most influential writer, without a doubt, is Jessica Mitford," said Jk Rowling. "When my grand-aunt gave me Hons and Rebels when I was 14, she instantly became my heroine. She ran away from home to fight in the Spanish Civil War, taking with her a camera that she had charged to her father's account. I wished I'd had the nerve to do something like that. I love the way she never outgrew some of her adolescent traits, remaining true to her politics — she was a self-taught socialist — throughout her life. I think I've read everything she wrote. I even called my daughter Jessica Rowling Arantes after her."

(744) Production designer Stuart Craig says that designing the Room of Requirements for the films was a big challenge. "I like to think of every set as a sculpture in the first place, and that was a big challenge. We built a crude, simplistic model just in Styrofoam, and this was literally an abstract sculpture. Then that was translated into a much more detailed model with doll's furniture, which became the blueprint for the whole set. Then we went to every auction, every sale room for second hand furniture and so we made a big, physical set. And, finally, visual effects took all of that and made it that much bigger."

(745) You can purchase a Harry Potter Death Eaters Rising Board Game. 'He-Who-Must-Not-Be-Named has returned! Lord Voldemort and his Death Eaters are a mounting threat to Hogwarts and the wizarding community, compelling everyone to combine their strengths against the dark villains. In this cooperative game, players must summon witches and wizards from Dumbledore's Army, the Order of the Phoenix, and Hogwarts to retaliate against evil Death Eaters and protect the Wizarding World from the Dark Lord's corruption for good!'

(746) The name Quirinus Quirrell is inspired by Janus Quirinus - a two-headed Roman god of doors and beginnings.

(747) Slythern's wand was made of Snakewood and basilisk horn.

(748) Harry Potter wears Converse footwear in the later films.

(749) JK Rowling says that some of the names in Harry Potter were inspired by gravestones in Greyfriars Kirkyard - a graveyard she used to walk through in Edinburgh.

(750) Ron doesn't like corned beef sandwiches. Corned beef in Britain often comes in a tin with gelatin. It isn't really what you would call a delicacy.

(751) Cistem Aperio is the incantation of a charm to blast open a chest or box.

(752) JK Rowling pointed out another inspiration from the Legend of King Arthur on Harry Potter when she said - "There is a further allusion to Excalibur emerging from the lake when Harry must dive into a frozen forest pool to retrieve the sword in Deathly Hallows. In other versions of the legend, Excalibur was given to Arthur by the Lady of the Lake, and was returned to the lake when he died."

(753) The first print run of Harry Potter and the Philosopher's Stone was a paltry 1,000 copies.

(754) David Heyman says that all the Harry Potter directors were asked to come back again after they'd finished their respective films. Aside from Chris Columbus doing the second one, David Yates is the only person who took them up on the offer and kept going.

(755) David Yates said he couldn't bear the thought of someone else (a new director) coming in and finishing the series when it was so close to the end so he stayed on.

(756) JK Rowling wrote that - 'Lupin's condition of lycanthropy was a metaphor for those illnesses that carry a stigma, like HIV and AIDS. All kinds of superstitions seem to surround blood-borne conditions, probably due to taboos surrounding blood itself. The wizarding community is as prone to hysteria and prejudice as the Muggle one, and the character of Lupin gave me a chance to examine those attitudes.'

(757) You can buy a Harry Potter Trivial Pursuit (although it's not cheap!). The blurb goes like this - 'Harry Potter fans test their knowledge of all 8 Harry Potter movies with TRIVIAL PURSUIT: World of Harry Potter Ultimate Edition. Move around the board with House Mascot movers as you answer questions and collect "wedges". Includes 1800 questions to challenge the ultimate Harry Potter fan. Categories include: Slytherin House, Death Eaters & The Dark Arts, Animals, Magical Creatures & Magical Beings, Witches, Wizards, Ghosts & Muggles, Hogwarts, Other Locations & Transportation Spells, Potions & Other Magic.'

(758) JK Rowling released a rather alarming pice of trivia about Hogwarts in 2020. "Hogwarts didn't always have bathrooms. Before adopting Muggle plumbing methods in the eighteenth century, witches and wizards simply relieved themselves wherever they stood, and vanished the evidence."

(759) Orlando Ticket Deals recommend the Butterbeer at the Wizarding World of Harry Potter. 'A visit to the Wizarding World of Harry Potter isn't complete until you've tried the Butterbeer. Harry Potter fans will know that this drink is a popular choice with wizards (especially Harry, Ron and Hermione). Wondering what it tastes like? Butterbeer is a

deliciously sweet drink that tastes like a mixture of caramel, butterscotch and cream soda. You can also get frozen Butterbeer, which is perfect for cooling down from the Floridian sunshine.'

(760) Hagrid does not have a patronus.

(761) JK Rowling gave Harry a lightning scar because she thought it looked cool.

(762) Daniel Radcliffe said that when the Potter franchise ended and he worked on other projects, the crews were surprised to find that he was normal and down to earth. They had expected him to be a spoiled child star!

(763) Costume designer Jany Temime says that Daniel Radcliffe has no interest in clothes or fashion whatsoever.

(764) The Bird-Conjuring Charm (Avis) - as the name suggests - is a charm that produces a flock of birds.

(765) Harry Potter costume designer Jany Temime says she helped Emma Watson choose her red carpet dresses for the Hary Potter premieres.

(766) The Freezing Spell (Glacius) produces ice from the tip of a wand.

(767) Professor Snape's first words to Harry in the books ("What would I get if I added powdered root of asphodel to an infusion of wormwood?") have a hidden meaning. Asphodel is a type of lily and means 'my regrets follow you to the grave'. Wormwood is connected with regret and bitterness.

(768) Harry's plight and backstory in the first book clearly owes something to Cinderella.

(769) JK Rowling is quite dismayed when people try to interpret the Harry Potter books as conservative. "So I'm told repeatedly. The two groups of people who are constantly thanking me are Wiccans and boarding schools. And really, don't thank me. I'm not with either of them. New ageism leaves me completely cold, and [my daughter] would never go to boarding school. I went to a comprehensive."

(770) Harry Potter has inspired several hundred thousand pieces of fan fiction.

(771) JK Rowling says that "Harry is often given an erroneous first impression of somebody and he has to learn to look beneath the surface. When he looks beneath the surface, he has sometimes found that he has been fooled by people. On other occasions, he has found some nice surprises."

(772) Daniel Radcliffe says shooting the Quidditch scenes in the films were a pain because he had to sit on a broom all day pretending to fly.

(773) The Herbivicus Charm (Herbivicus) makes flowers and plants grow very rapidly.

(774) JK Rowling says she wished she had saved Dobby for the climatic battle.

(775) You can, should you wish, buy a 1000 piece Harry Potter jigsaw puzzle featuring the Hogwarts Express. 'Wave goodbye to Hagrid as you prepare to find platform 9 3/4 London to Hogwarts! Relive the excitement of Harry Potter with this 1000-piece Hogwarts Express jigsaw puzzle. Ideal for lovers of the movies and books alike.'

(776) JK Rowling says that once the sense of relief had evaporated, she felt a great sense of sadness at finishing the last book. "It was a bereavement. We know the people we love

are immortal. We know we are immortal. So I knew the whole thing. I even knew how it'll end. So when it ended, I was in a slight state of shock. There came a point where I cried. It was only once I cried once before, when my mother died. It (Harry Potter) had stayed with me for 17 years and then it just ended. It was happening when I was going through a very tumultuous time personally. If it can be an escape for these children, then you can imagine what it would have been like for me. And not just an escape to that world. It disciplined me as a writer, and gave structure to my life. I knew I would be writing. But I had to mourn Harry."

(777) Ravenclaw's mascot is an eagle.

(778) Regarding the use of Latin in the Harry Potter books, JK Rowling says - "I take great liberties with the language for spells because I see it as a mutation that the wizards are using."

(779) Draco is the only student whom Snape addresses by his first name.

(780) Costume designer Jany Temime says that Evanna Lynch was the biggest real life Harry Potter fan out of the young cast members in the films. "Evanna Lynch, she was a Potter freak. She knew everything about Harry Potter. They gave her extensions in hair and make-up, and she would go home and sleep in her extensions. She didn't want to take them off. She was really Luna. She loved the Christmas tree dress. She was making jewelry with me. She helped me with the lion head. She was very involved."

(781) Film Fiction ranked Harry Potter and the Chamber of Secrets as the best of the Potter video games. 'Don't pretend you didn't see this coming, every fan knows that this is the best Harry Potter game, ever! This took everything that had made Philosopher's Stone work and improved on it. I just

loved how this game opened up Hogwarts to you and the world you're in, it felt like you were playing 'Grand Theft Potter', you could fly anywhere on your broomstick, there were a lot of collectibles to find and it had a lot of Zelda like elements to it for unlocking spells to go to different areas and simple RPG elements as well. This truly was a Harry Potter game done right.'

(782) JK Rowling says that Harry would have fought for Snape's portrait to be hung in Hogwarts next to that of Dumbledore.

(783) Green is the colour of Slytherin.

(784) When he was asked what distinguished his version of Dumbledore from Richard Harris, Michael Gambon said - "I'm a little bit more camp, I think, a bit lighter. A bit more ethereal."

(785) Dolores Umbridge was based on a real person JK Rowling knew. There was no love lost between them.

(786) Costume designer Jany Temime says she loved designing the costumes for Helena Bonham Carter as Bellatrix the most.

(787) Orlando Ticket Deals had this to say about the Otter's Fizzy Orange Juice you can buy at the Wizarding World of Harry Potter - 'For those of you who don't fancy branching out to the Fishy Green Ale, this is a safe (but delicious!) option. This fizzy orange drink has a hint of vanilla, and is the perfect refreshing drink for when you need a break from all that theme park fun. The sugar and cinnamon coated rim totally transforms the flavour and compliments the fresh orange juice. We're sure you'll love it as much as we do!'

(788) JK Rowling says she has always loved the concept of

magic. "There are certain themes within the books that are perennial and recurrent, particularly in children's literature. I've always said I think the appeal of magic is particularly profound to children because of their powerlessness. The idea that you would be given extra powers and be able to organize the universe according to your plan — or just your little world according to your wishes — is enormously appealing."

(789) Daniel Radcliffe is said to have earned $20 million for each of the Deathly Hallows movies.

(790) Harry Potter games and toys are estimated to have made about $8 billion.

(791) Scholastic purchased the American publishing rights to Harry Potter from JK Rowling for $105,000 after reading Philosopher's Stone.

(792) Emma Watson is a certified yoga teacher.

(793) Costume designer Jany Temime says her approach to dressing the Weasley twins [James and Oliver Phelps] was - "I would do it not the same but complimentary. So when was one in stripes, the other one was in squares with the same colours. Or when one had vertical stripes, the other one had horizontal stripes, because I thought it was funnier to do something complimentary than something exactly the same."

(794) Arabella Figg is actually a squib. A Squib is someone who was born into a wizarding family but hasn't got any magic powers.

(795) In a 2011 Bloomsbury poll, Snape was voted the favourite character in Harry Potter. He took 20% of the 70,000 votes cast.

(796) The script for Harry Potter and the Cursed Child was the

highest-selling print book of 2016.

(797) The staff at the Wizarding World of Harry Potter are tested on their Harry Potter knowledge before being hired.

(798) Emma Watson, at 15, was the youngest person to be on the cover of Teen Vogue magazine.

(799) The Invisibility Cloak was created by Ignotus Peverell, a 13th-century wizard who eluded death by wearing it.

(800) Among the grumps who gave the first Harry Potter book a bad review was Harold Bloom in the Wall Street Journal. "One can reasonably doubt that Harry Potter and the Sorcerer's Stone is going to prove a classic of children's literature, but Rowling, whatever the aesthetic weaknesses of her work, is at least a millennial index to our popular culture. Her prose style, heavy on cliche, makes no demands upon her readers. In an arbitrarily chosen single page — page 4 — of the first Harry Potter book, I count seven cliches, all of the 'stretch his legs' variety. How to read Harry Potter and the Sorcerer's Stone? Why, very quickly, to begin with, perhaps also to make an end. Why read it? Presumably, if you cannot be persuaded to read anything better, Rowling will have to do."

(801) Anthony Holden in the Guardian also seemed irked at Potter mania. "These are one-dimensional children's books, Disney cartoons written in words, no more. We are a country with dramatically declining standards of literacy, increasingly dragged down to the lowest common denominator by the purveyors of all forms of mindless mass entertainment. The success of the Potter books is just another dispiriting proof of the Murdoch-led dumbing down of all our lives, or what Hensher called 'the infantilisation of adult culture'.

What I do object to is a pedestrian, ungrammatical prose style which has left me with a headache and a sense of a wasted opportunity. If Rowling is blessed with this magic gift of tapping into young minds, I can only wish she had made better use of it. Her characters, unlike life's, are all black-and-white. Her story-lines are predictable, the suspense minimal, the sentimentality cloying every page. Did Harry, like so many child-heroes before him, HAVE to be yet another poignant orphan?"

(802) Harry Potter and the Deathly Hallows Part 2 is the highest rated of the movies on Rotten Tomatoes with 97%.

(803) Reparo is the Mending Charm. This is very useful if you need to tidy up a house or have broken your favourite cup!

(804) When the film series concluded, Robbie Coltrane said that "something strangely wonderful" had come to an end.

(805) During an infamous Quidditch match in the year 1473, all 700 Quidditch fouls were made.

(806) Harry Potter and the Chamber of Secrets is titled Harry Potter and the Secret Room in Japanese.

(807) Deathly Hallows Part 1 suffered from a leak before its cinema release. Thirty-six minutes of the film was illegally posted on the web.

(808) Mastermind, a long running quiz show in Britain, banned contestants from choosing Harry Potter as their specialised subject because it had been chosen on the show too many times already.

(809) "To invent this wizard world, I've learned a ridiculous amount about alchemy," said JK Rowling in 1998.

(810) When the films ended, Helen Bonham Carter took home the fake dentures she wore as Bellatrix as a memento.

(811) Harry Potter and the Philosopher's Stone is called Harry Potter and the Stone of the Wise Men in Dutch.

(812) Hermione's wand is made out of vine wood with a core of dragon heartstring.

(813) Rictusempra is the tickling charm.

(814) The BBC website gave Harry Potter and the Philosopher's Stone 4 out of 5 when the film was released in 2001. 'Possibly Hollywood's first bespectacled hero since Harold Lloyd, Harry Potter makes a satisfactory, albeit unspectacular, celluloid debut in Chris Columbus' $125 million movie about the young boy destined to be a great wizard.

Treating JK Rowling's debut novel with a reverence that wasn't even accorded to The Bible, Hollywood serves up a two-and-a-half hour fantasy that gets the introductions out of the way, paving the way for more plot-driven tales in what's sure to become the biggest franchise of all time. (On the big screen, incidentally, the story's similarities to Star Wars are even more pronounced.) If you've read the novel - and if you haven't, why not? - impeccable casting means you'll feel like you've met all of these characters already. The three young leads - Radcliffe, Grint, and especially Watson - deliver likable, natural performances, while the film's biggest joy is watching the spot-on performances of their peers: Maggie Smith plays Professor McGonagall like Miss Jean Brodie with a pointy hat, while Robbie Coltrane steals the show as loose-lipped Hagrid. Alan Rickman, meanwhile, sneers for England as Professor Snape. Indeed, the whole film plays like an advertisement for historic old England - if this doesn't get Americans buying our castles and cathedrals, or at least coming to look at them again, nothing will. Hell, even King's Cross station looks pleasant. The film's not flawless, though.

It's half an hour too long and much of the book's humour is jettisoned. Still, it's refreshing to witness a big-budget movie where the impressive special effects complement the story, rather than merely compensate for the lack of one. Harry Potter may not leave you spellbound, then, but it'll definitely leave you wanting to discover the Chamber of Secrets.'

(815) In a 2011 MTV poll, Dobby was voted the best magical creature with an overwhelming 54% of the vote.

(816) In a YouGov survey, 15% of Americans said that the Harry Potter series was a bad influence on children because it portrayed witchcraft.

(817) Durham University in England introduced a module where students can study the social, cultural and educational context of Harry Potter.

(818) Petrificus Totalus is the Full Body Curse. This will make someone unable to move (and probably fall over).

(819) Harry Potter and the Deathly Hallows is called Harry Potter and the Talismans of Death in Norwegian.

(820) Julie Walters, who is quite small and petite, wore padding in the films to make Mrs Weasley feel more 'motherly' and plumpish.

(821) JK Rowling says that Mad-Eye moody turned out a lot better than she expected. 'It was a big surprise to me that Mad-Eye Moody turned out the way he did. I really like him. I didn't expect to.'

(822) Ginny went on to become a professional Quidditch player for the Holyhead Harpies.

(823) Paste Magazine ranked Harry Potter: Quidditch World

Cup as the best video game based on Harry Potter. 'You knew this was coming. Like a Bludger out of Hell, Quidditch World Cup managed to condense the most entertaining aspect of any Harry Potter game into one standalone title. Combining the thrill of jockeying for position against enemy Seekers, scoring high-flying goals as a Chaser, and unlocking additional abilities with collectable cards and in-game challenges, the game had very little chance at losing the interest of its youthful audience, especially when playing against friends. There's no doubt in my mind that the game played a key role in inspiring numerous real world Quidditch leagues across college campuses everywhere. If there's one legacy worth keeping in the gaming world, it's that your product becomes real life through an endless reserve of fandom.'

(824) The huge success of the Potter franchise led to film studios taking a huge interest in YA fiction in the hope of finding the next Harry Potter type phenomenon. The Hunger Games, The Maze Runner, Divergent, Inkheart, The Spiderwick Chroniches, and Eragon (amongst many others) all found their way to the screen.

(825) An anagram of Remus Lupin is primus lune - Latin for first moon.

(826) Snape was inspired by JK Rowling's secondary school chemistry teacher John Nettleship.

(827) When the first film came out in Britain, Peter Smith, general secretary of the Association of Teachers and Lecturers, managed to get himself in the news by warning about the themes of Harry Potter. "Increasing numbers of children are spending hours alone browsing the Internet in search of satanic websites. ATL is concerned that nobody is monitoring this growing fascination. The surge in interest in the occult is, at its best, a welcome stimulus to children's imagination and personal growth. Children, particularly girls on the cusp of

puberty, have always been interested in magic and in parallel worlds. Casting spells gives them a feeling of control over an increasingly confusing world at a time when many youngsters feel powerless. But there is a darker side to the occult which may disturb vulnerable children and expose them to manipulation by adults. Parents and teachers will want to educate young people about the dangers of dabbling in the occult, before they become too deeply involved. The Harry Potter movie will lead to a whole new generation of youngsters discovering witchcraft and wizardry. We welcome the values this will ingrain, focusing on good triumphing over evil. Though it is important not to over-react to this fun and entertaining phenomenon, the risks are clear. Children must be protected from the more extreme influences of the occult and be taught in a responsible and positive way the risks of journeying into the unknown."

(828) In a 2011 YouGov survey, 25% of Americans said they had seen all of the Harry Potter movies.

(829) There are a number of 'goofs' in the films for the eagle-eyed. In Harry Potter and the Prisoner of Azkaban for example, you can see the 'battery packs' underneath the clothing of Daniel Radcliffe and Emma Watson in some of the outdoor scenes. This equipment is common in the film industry and used to make actors voices easier to hear and record.

(830) JK Rowling has said that "I am not a great fan of fantasy books in general, and never read them!"

(831) The famous film critic Roger Ebert gave the first film a glowing review when it came out. 'Harry Potter and the Sorcerer's Stone is a red-blooded adventure movie, dripping with atmosphere, filled with the gruesome and the sublime, and surprisingly faithful to the novel. A lot of things could have gone wrong, and none of them have: Chris Columbus'

movie is an enchanting classic that does full justice to a story that was a daunting challenge. The novel by JK Rowling was muscular and vivid, and the danger was that the movie would make things too cute and cuddly. It doesn't. Like an Indiana Jones for younger viewers, it tells a rip-roaring tale of supernatural adventure, where colourful and eccentric characters alternate with scary stuff like a three-headed dog, a pit of tendrils known as the Devil's Snare and a two-faced immortal who drinks unicorn blood. Scary, yes, but not too scary--just scary enough. During Harry Potter and the Sorcerer's Stone, I was pretty sure I was watching a classic, one that will be around for a long time, and make many generations of fans. It takes the time to be good. It doesn't hammer the audience with easy thrills, but cares to tell a story, and to create its characters carefully.'

(832) Harry Potter and the Deathly Hallows is called Harry Potter and the Gifts of Death in Albanian.

(833) Disney bid for the Harry Potter film rights but did not get them because JK Rowling felt they wanted too much creative control. She wanted to retain some input into any films made from the books. Disney must have greatly regretted this later because they couldn't use Harry Potter in their theme parks.

(834) JK Rowling said that the Malfoys used to hobnob with rich and important muggles - like royalty for example.

(835) Xenophilius translates as 'lover of strange things' in Greek.

(836) Cho Chang married a muggle.

(837) Robbie Coltrane's costume as the Spirit of Christmas in the 1988 comedy special Blackadder's Christmas Carol feels very similar to Hagrid. Many speculate then that JK Rowling

watched this and always had the image of Robbie Coltrane from Blackadder in her head when she created Hagrid. It would certainly explain why she insisted he had to play the part in the films.

(838) Dumbledore's first name is Albus. Albus is Latin for white.

(839) The word Muggle is now in the Oxford English Dictionary. It is described as 'a person who lacks a particular skill or skills, or who is regarded as inferior in some way'.

(840) Amy H Sturgis, an assistant professor of liberal studies at Lenoir-Rhyne University, says of the appeal of Harry Potter that - "Children and adults can see themselves in the stories. The moral dilemmas, the decisions that Harry and his friends are faced with, the big themes of doing what is right, not what is easy — these are timeless. Everyone can identify with them. It's not a story that has a limited shelf life."

(841) JK Rowling chose the name Hermione because it was a very uncommon name that few girls in real life had.

(842) In a YouGov poll, 45% of Americans said the Harry Potter series of books and films was entertaining but had no important life lessons.

(843) Alfonso Cuaron said of his experience directing Harry Potter and the Prisoner of Azkaban that "I stepped into a machine that was so well put together, so wealthy and safe. It was like I was invited to cook a meal, and in the kitchen all the tools are there."

(844) Kevin Fiege has said that the Harry Potter films were an influence on the Marvel universe. The Potter films showed you could could have a huge story arc across several movies.

(845) Entertainment Direct ranked Harry Potter and the Chamber of Secrets as the best Harry Potter video game. This was, for those who were counting, the second Harry Potter video game ever released. 'The second Harry Potter game ever released also remains the best Harry Potter adventure, in terms of character portrayals, gameplay, and pure, unadulterated fun. Players are expected to take control of Harry himself while exploring Hogwarts and its surrounding areas, all while attending classes and completing a vast array of challenges. Simplistic as it is, the game manages to include intriguing aspects such as a broomstick free-flight mode, engaging mini-games, and quests based on real events players would have read about in the books. If you're looking for ways to get even closer to the world of Harry Potter, these games are your best ticket to Hogwarts. Have fun playing (but be sure to check-in with the Muggles around you every once in a while).'

(846) There are 493 Knuts to a Galleon.

(847) Harry Potter and the Deathly Hallows sold 8 million copies in 24 hours.

(848) Herpo the Foul was the original creator of the horcrux.

(849) Harry Potter and the Prisoner of Azkaban is called Harry Potter and the Escapee from Azkaban in Chinese.

(850) The New York Times gave the first Harry Potter film a slightly sniffy review when it came out. 'The most highly awaited movie of the year has a dreary, literal-minded competence, following the letter of the law as laid down by the author. But it's all muted flourish, with momentary pleasures, like Gringott's, the bank staffed by trolls that looks like a Gaudí throwaway. The picture is so careful that even the tape wrapped around the bridge of Harry's glasses seems to have come out of the set design. The movie comes across as

a covers act by an extremely competent tribute band -- not the real thing but an incredible simulation. This overly familiar movie is like a theme park that's a few years past its prime; the rides clatter and groan with metal fatigue every time they take a curve. The picture's very raggedness makes it spooky, which is not the same thing as saying the movie is intentionally unsettling.'

(851) Protego is a shield charm that will cause minor jinxes or hexes to bounce back to the person who cast it.

(852) A YouGov survey in Britain saw Hermione Granger voted the best character. Dumbledore was second and Harry was third.

(853) Harry Potter and the Philosopher's Stone is called Harry Potter and the Wisdom's Stone in Lithuanian.

(854) Between 3,000 and 4,000 people worked in some capacity on each Harry Potter film.

(855) In a YouGov survey, 39% of Americans said that Harry Potter was a good influence and had positive lessons to teach.

(856) Tom Felton also auditioned to play Ron.

(857) JK Rowling says that the muggle sport which Quidditch most resembles is Basketball.

(858) You can now buy a Bulbbotz Harry Potter Alarm Clock. 'Become a powerful wizard with the Bulbbotz Harry Potter Night Light Alarm Clock. Join Harry as he leads Dumbledore's Army to victory with his night light functions, easy to read LCD display and alarm settings. Press down on his sound button to reveal his character sound effects. A fun night light for even the darkest hour, this fun digital alarm clock is a must for every Harry Potter fan!'

(859) In a 2013 interview, Daniel Radcliffe said "I do not miss playing Harry Potter or feel nostalgic. Starting afresh, going on to a set not knowing anyone, that's fun and exciting."

(860) Peter Bradshaw gave Deathly Hallows Part 1 a middling review in the Guardian. 'Just as before, there is a good 90-minute story visible inside this highly decorated circus elephant of a film. An experimental, low-budget version of Harry Potter (and what unthinkable commercial heresy that would be) might feature only Harry, Ron and Hermione roaming in various Beckettian wildernesses, seedy urban bars and deserted Orwellian ministerial corridors, arguing ceaselessly among themselves. And yet it is only when these three are on their own that this film comes to life: especially in the eerie Forest of Dean or a gloomy Shaftesbury Avenue cafe in central London where they have a magic-wand shootout with two assassins.'

(861) Harry Potter and the Deathly Hallows Part 1 is the lowest rated of the Harry Potter movies on Rotten Tomatoes with (a still perfectly respectable) 77%.

(862) A YouGov survey in America voted the Summoning Charm as the most popular spell.

(863) The British Medical Journal reported that whenever a new Harry Potter book was released there were less incidences of children being taken to hospitals for bumps and scrapes and injuries through sports and playing outside. Most children were safely at home reading Harry Potter!

(864) JK Rowling's handprints were reproduced on flagstone in front of the Edinburgh City Chambers after she was awarded the Edinburgh Award in 2008 for her contributions to the city.

(865) You can now purchase a Harry Potter Pictopia Game. The blurbs goes like this - 'Showcase your knowledge of J. K. Rowling's wizarding world when you encounter 1,000 picture trivia questions featuring the beloved characters, extraordinary places, magical creatures and enchanted objects from the epic Harry Potter films. It's a game of teamwork with a competitive twist!'

(866) A Time Magazine survey found that most Americans thought of themselves as natural Ravenclaws.

(867) Nicolas Flamel has a fountain at the Beauxbatons Academy of Magic.

(868) The tongue flick of Bartemius Crouch Jr in the films was an improvisation of David Tennant.

(869) Harry Potter and the Deathly Hallows is called Harry Potter and the Relics of Death in German.

(870) JK Rowling says she doesn't like illustrations in text books for children because she think it's much better to use your imagination.

(871) Appare Vestigium is the tracking spell. One can use this to deduce footprints.

(872) The Elder Wand's core is a thestral tail hair.

(873) In a YouGov survey, 54% of people in Britain said they would choose Hufflepuff out of the Hogwarts Houses.

(874) The Scotsman newspaper gave the first Harry Potter book a very positive review in 1997. 'If you buy or borrow nothing else this summer for the young readers in your family, you must get hold of a copy of Harry Potter and the Philosopher's Stone by JK Rowley [sic]. This is a book which

makes an unassailable stand for the power of fresh, inventive storytelling in the face of formula horror and sickly romance. The story of the book's origins is a fairy tale all of its own. This first novel from an Edinburgh-based author has just received a six-figure advance in America. Yet it was written in snatches by an unemployed single mother. Joanne Rowling arrived in Edinburgh penniless following the break-up of her marriage. The book took shape as she scribbled feverishly in cafes as soon as her baby daughter dropped off to sleep in her pushchair. The fairy tale ending is now complete, with money and critical praise being showered on the adventures of young Harry. The sequel is already nearly completed. In the first book, we hear of Harry's early years, which following the death of his parents have been spent in Dickensian misery at the hands of his horrible aunt and uncle. But help is at hand and despite all manner of obstacles, he soon finds himself on platform nine-and-three-quarters at Waterloo Station, from which the train for Hogwarts School of Wizardry and Witchcraft departs. What distinguishes this novel from so many other fantasies is its grip on reality. Harry is a hugely likeable child, kind but not wet, competitive but always compassionate. The scene in which he thwarts a bully's attempt to unseat him from his broomstick during an exacting game of Quidditch - a cross between lacrosse and hockey, played on land and in the air - will ring bells with the most level-headed of readers. He has much to live up to. His parents were both respected and much loved. The wizard who killed them, an individual so ghastly that his name can never be uttered, remains at large and a constant threat, and there are deliciously tense and frightening moments. Rowling uses classic narrative devices with flair and originality and delivers a complex and demanding plot to create a hugely entertaining thriller. She is a first-rate writer for children.'

(875) Ariana Grande said she was put in Slytherin by Pottermore's sorting hat quiz.

(876) The eight original Harry Potter films didn't win a single Oscar in any category - a snub which seemed to somewhat baffle and annoy the people who made them. However in 2017, Fantastic Beasts and Where to Find Them did win the Academy Award for Best Achievement in Costume Design.

(877) The broomstick props in the Potter films are made from lightweight aluminum.

(878) JK Rowling says that her favorite sweets in Harry Potter would have to be chocolate frogs.

(879) You can now buy Harry Potter Scrabble from the Harry Potter shop. 'An enchanting twist on the traditional word game, SCRABBLE: World of Harry Potter puts your knowledge of the Wizarding World to the test. Strategically play both regular words and your favorite Harry Potter words to score high. Customize your game with Harry Potter cards and Magical Bonus cards to score even higher and win the game!'

(880) You can, should you wish, now buy a cardboard cutout of Ron Weasely. 'Bring the magic of the Wizarding World home today. With this brilliant Harry Potter party cardboard cutout of Ron Weaseley you are sure to create the atmosphere you want easily whatever the event. Surprise the fan in your life with a lifesize cut out of their favourite character. Guests and fans will delight in the opportunity to be pictured with their hero.'

(881) Ron was partly inspired by JK Rowling's friend Sean Harris. Rowling said that "Ron has a Sean-ish turn of phrase."

(882) Front Row Reviews gave Harry Potter and the Deathly Hallows Part 2 a very positive review. 'It's not a perfect feature but at this stage it would seem churlish to criticise a film that marks the end of an era both in literature and

cinema. The books and films have opened up millions of hearts and minds to imagination, wonder and the value of friendship, loyalty and love and that translates to the screen here. No film in the series has ever felt so infused with passion or emotion and one feels the emotions on screen during the final battle likely echo those off. Harry's glasses have broken countless times, Ron's fainted tedious times – and even thrown up slugs – and Hermione's relentlessly answered questions no one even asked. But for all their idiosyncrasies we've taken to these characters, this place, and this world, you could say, as if by magic. As those on the side of good stand together it's impossible not to be moved to stand with them and as goodbyes go it's a triumphant send off for the most beloved and successful children's story of all time. Move over Azkaban, because Potter and co have saved the best till last.'

(883) Alfonso Cuaron had an idea for a sequence in Harry Potter and the Prisoner of Azkaban where Hogwarts had some little tiny people who could jump up and down on piano keys. JK Rowling didn't like this idea at all and vetoed the planned scene.

(884) The wizarding school Durmstrang is thought to be in Sweden or Norway.

(885) One of Dumbledore's middle names is Wulfric. Wulfric (died circa 1004) was an Anglo-Saxon nobleman. His will is an important document from the reign of King Æthelred the Unready. Wulfric was a patron of the Burton Abbey, around which the modern town of Burton on Trent later grew up, and may have refounded the Benedictine monastery there.

(886) Fans of Asterix often wonder if Dumbledore was influenced by Getafix.

Asterix first appeared in Pilote magazine in 1959 and has since been translated into 100 languages, selling over 300 million books. The series revolves around a sleepy village by the sea in ancient Gaul (a region of Western Europe during the Iron Age and Roman era which included France - where Asterix is set) that steadfastly refuses to acknowledge Roman rule because they have a magic potion brewed by their venerable druid Getafix that gives the recipient super strength. So any Romans with designs on the village can expect a magic potion enhanced bashing. Despite the invaders controlling the outside world (save for the surrounding forest - which the Gauls consider their own private domain) life there amongst the little thatched huts goes on as normal with bickering, banquets, hunting, mass brawls, friendships, gossip, rivalries, celebrations. The Asterix series was a perfect unison between the talented and amusing artist Albert Uderzo and the equally talented and amusing writer René Goscinny. Asterix was surrounded with memorable supporting characters and this was always a huge part of the appeal of the books. From his portly boar munching menhir obsessed best friend Obelix to the long suffering Chief Vitalstatistix (who always insisted on being carried around on a shield and frequently got dropped) to Getafix (Panoramix in the French version) the wise druid. Getafix is one of the greatest characters in the world of Asterix and like a cross between Gandalf and a hippy with his huge beard, white robes and golden sickle. Getafix is a humanist and provides moral guidance in the village. He is like everyone's grandfather. The Gauls might be near invulnerable with their potion but they are a superstitious bunch and greatly fear the day when the sky might fall on their heads so their druid is always a reassuring presence, as of course is his magic potion, the secret of which is "lost in the mists of time..." Getafix is definitely the Dumbledore of the village in Asterix.

(887) Lavender Brown was played by three different actresses in the films. The explanation for the recasting is that they wanted a more experienced actress later on when the character became more important. Jessie Cave was cast for this reason.

(888) JK Rowling considered the first names Pi and Digit for Septima Vector, the Arithmancy professor.

(889) Collider ranked Harry Potter and the Prisoner of Azkaban as the best of the movies and Harry Potter and the Chamber of Secrets as the weakest.

(890) A YouGov survey in 2011 found that 31% of Americans had read at least one Harry Potter book.

(891) Hogwarts wizards use cauldrons. While still used for cooking, a more common association is the cauldron's use in witchcraft for works of fiction.

(892) In the Worst Witch books by Jill Murphy, the children have flying broomstick lessons. Sound familiar?

(893) Grawp was originally going to be Hagrid's cousin.

(894) Rupert Grint said of Harry Potter and the Cursed Child - "I saw the play, Harry Potter and the Cursed Child. It was very strange. It was almost like an out-of-body experience. But yeah, it was incredible seeing it move on, and seeing someone else's interpretation of it as well was really interesting. I really enjoyed it."

(895) Stephen King loves the Harry Potter books and says they were a great comfort to him when he was recovering from a bad accident. 'I read the first novel in the Harry Potter series, Harry Potter and the Sorcerer's Stone, in April 1999 and was only moderately impressed. But in April 1999 I was pretty much all right. Two months later I was involved in a serious road accident that necessitated a long and painful period of recuperation. During the early part of this period I read Potters 2 and 3 (Chamber of Secrets, Prisoner of Azkaban) and found myself a lot more than moderately wowed. In the

miserably hot summer of '99, the Harry Potters (and the superb detective novels of Dennis Lehane) became a kind of lifeline for me. During July and August I found myself getting through my unpleasant days by aiming my expectations at evening, when I would drag my hardware-encumbered leg into the kitchen, eat fresh fruit and ice cream and read about Harry Potter's adventures at Hogwarts, a school for young wizards (motto: 'Never tickle a sleeping dragon').

(896) Stephen King said he understood the sadness of fans when the book series came to an end. 'When it comes to Harry, part of me, a fairly large part, actually, can hardly bear to say goodbye. I'd guess that JK Rowling feels the same, although I'd also guess those feelings are mingled with the relief of knowing that the work is finally done, for better or worse. And I'm a grown-up, for God's sake, a damn Muggle! Think how it must be for all the kids who were 8 when Harry debuted in Harry Potter and the Philosopher's Stone, with its cartoon jacket and modest (500 copies) first edition. Those kids are now 18, and when they close the final book, they will be in some measure closing the book on their own childhoods - magic summers spent in the porch swing, or reading under the covers at camp with flashlights in hand, or listening to Jim Dale's recordings on long drives to see Grandma in Cincinnati or Uncle Bob in Wichita. My advice to families containing Harry Potter readers: Stock up on the Kleenex. You're gonna need it. It's all made worse by one unavoidable fact: It's not just Harry. It's time to say goodbye to the whole cast, from Moaning Myrtle to Scabbers the rat (a.k.a. Wormtail).'

(897) Quietus is the Quietening Charm. This would be useful in a library!

(898) Richard Griffiths, who played Vernon Dursley, also appeared in the play Equus with Daniel Radcliffe.

(899) Richard Griffiths passed away in 2013. "Richard was by

my side during two of the most important moments of my career," said Daniel Radcliffe. "Any room he walked into was made twice as funny and twice as clever just by his presence. I am proud to say I knew him."

(900) Ian Hart, who played Professor Quirrell, seemed to suggest that he wasn't paid much money to be in Harry Potter. "Warner Bros – I'm not going to slag them off – it was a long time ago now, but what Zoe Wanamaker said about the pay, knowing that they were going to make a fortune, they were still paying you as if you were just a trivial English actor, and for brokering that notion on television and in the press, I don't think she was invited back for the other films. What I'm trying to say is, that everyone was cosy and loads of people made a ton of money, but I didn't. Even in the first film, I had no leverage, because I wasn't in the next fourteen films, so I had no leverage. I knew I was dead. They paid me and let me go. That was fine, I enjoyed it. I had a good time and I enjoyed it, so I have no complaints."

(901) The scenes in Harry Potter and the Philosopher's Stone where Harry learns that he can speak to snakes where shot at the Reptile House of London Zoo.

(902) JK Rowling thought about killing off Ron in the books but then decided against it.

(903) When he'd finished his final scene as Snape, Alan Rickman wrote a letter to Empire film magazine. 'I have just returned from the dubbing studio where I spoke into a microphone as Severus Snape for absolutely the last time. On the screen were some flashback shots of Daniel, Emma, and Rupert from ten years ago. They were 12. I have also recently returned from New York, and while I was there, I saw Daniel singing and dancing (brilliantly) on Broadway. A lifetime seems to have passed in minutes. Three children have become adults since a phone call with Jo Rowling, containing one

small clue, persuaded me that there was more to Snape than an unchanging costume, and that even though only three of the books were out at that time, she held the entire massive but delicate narrative in the surest of hands. It is an ancient need to be told in stories. But the story needs a great storyteller. Thanks for all of it, Jo.'

(904) Daniel Radcliffe's scream after the death of Sirius was cut out of the film franchise because it was deemed a bit too horrifying for a children's movie.

(905) The last scene of Harry Potter and the Philosopher's Stone was the first scene shot for the film.

(906) Dumbledore is an old English word for "bumblebee".

(907) In a 2011 MTV poll, Hermione's time turner was voted the best magical device in Harry Potter.

(908) The Grand Staircase of the Hogwarts in the films, with its impossible angles, was inspired by the works of the artist M.C. Escher.

(909) Hermione, in Greek mythology, was the daughter of Helen of Troy and Menelaus, king of Sparta.

(910) JK Rowling says she considered having Neville kill Bellatrix.

(911) Chris Columbus said of the first two films that "Casting these kids at the beginning of Sorcerer's Stone was, in a way, horrifying. I spent the first two weeks on that film trying to get them to look away from the camera, stop smiling and be able to utter one line so I could cut around it. When we wrapped on Chamber of Secrets, their performances had improved immensely, and they had become seasoned professionals."

(912) Dragon blood can be used as a spot remover.

(913) Magic Guidebooks say that the Pumpkin Juice for sale at the Wizarding World of Harry Potter in Universal Studios Orlando tastes like apple juice with cinnamon, nutmeg, and sugar.

(914) Glen Coe in Scotland was used for many outdoor sequences in the Harry Potter film franchise.

(915) Steven Spielberg said that one of the reasons why he decided not to make the first Harry Potter film was that he didn't consider it to be a big enough challenge. "I purposely didn't do the Harry Potter movie because for me, that was shooting ducks in a barrel. It's just a slam dunk. It's just like withdrawing a billion dollars and putting it into your personal bank accounts. There's no challenge."

(916) The name Hagrid might have been inspired by Thomas Hardy's novel The Mayor Of Casterbridge - which mentions 'Hag-rids'.

(917) An alternative explanation for Hagrid's name could be the term 'Hagridden' - which means to be worried or tormented by a witch.

(918) Emma Watson said that, when reading the books, she cried the most when Dobby died.

(919) In a YouGov poll, only 6% of Americans said they would want to be in Slytherin.

(920) Harry Potter and the Order of the Phoenix debuted on a record number of screens and 22,000 prints of the film raced around the world.

(921) Voldemort is correctly pronounced without the 't' at the end, as in 'Voldemore'.

(922) The Venomous Tentacula is considered as the perfect weapon to use against a Death Eater.

(923) Steve kloves, who wrote most of the Harry Potter films, says of Dumbledore - "I think Dumbledore's a fascinating character because I think he obviously sort of imparts great wisdom that comes from experience, but I've always felt that Dumbledore bears such a tremendous Dark burden, and he knows secrets and I think in many ways he bears the weight of the future of the wizard world, which is being challenged, and the only way that he can keep that at bay, the darkness, is to be whimsical and humorous. And I think that's just a really interesting thing, I think he's a character of so many layers and I think when he does say, that it is our choices and not our abilities. I just coming from him it doesn't feel like a sermon, it doesn't feel like a message, it just feels like an absolute truth and it goes down easy. And I like that about him. But that's what I like about the books, I've always said that I thought that Jo's writing is deceptively profound, which is that you never feel there are messages in there, but there's a lot of things being dealt with in a very sort of clever way, and they're never pretentious, the books, and I think that's why kids love reading them."

(924) Kloves said of the Harry Potter books - "I have two children and both grew up with Harry Potter in many ways. When you have children, when you're a new parent, you read LOADS of children's fiction. Most of it is, shall we say, lacking. It feels written down to some perceived lower level of understanding. It's the literary equivalent of Gerber creamed carrots. Except possessing no literary nourishment. Soft. Gooey. Jo's books were never that. In fact, they never felt like children's books. Consequently children--boys and girls-- embraced them eagerly. The books felt like proper books."

(925) Matthew Lewis had to sign a studio contract which banned him getting his teeth straightened for ten years while he played Neville.

(926) The writers of Avengers: Endgame say that the time travel plot (used to defeat Thanos) was inspired by the Time Turner in the Harry Potter films.

(927) Number 4 Privet Drive is named 12 Picket Post Close in real life. Winkfield Row in Bracknell was used before a set was built.

(928) The Cruciatus Curse is the second Unforgivable Curse. This inflicts great pain.

(929) Some of the portraits on the wall of Hogwarts in the film franchise actually depict the movie producers.

(930) There is a Roman goddess named Minerva.

(931) JK Rowling said that Snape was one of favourite characters to write but she would not want to meet him in real life.

(932) Hagrid's first name Rubeus comes from the Latin rubinius - which means red.

(933) The great hall set in the films was so large that you could fit over twenty double-decker buses in the space.

(934) In a 2011 MTV poll, Neville Longbottom was voted the character that most fans want to see in a spin-off film.

(935) Alan Rickman said that it wasn't quite true that he knew Snape's story arc right from the start thanks to JK Rowling but he says he was given a clue which helped to inform the

character. "Certainly, I did say I needed to talk to her before I could get a handle on how to play it, and we did have a phone conversation. She certainly didn't tell me what the end of the story was going to be in any way at all, so I was having to buy the books along with everybody else to find out, 'And now what?' No, she gave me one little piece of information, which I always said I would never share with anybody and never have, and never will. It wasn't a plot point, or crucial in any tangible way, but it was crucial to me as a piece of information that made me travel down that road rather than that one or that one or that one."

(936) It is estimated that there are millions of copies of fraudulent Harry Potter novels circulating in China. One book, titled Harry Potter and Bao Zoulong, simply reprinted The Hobbit and changed all the names to Harry Potter characters! The publishing house responsible had to pay a fine and offer an apology.

(937) An Indian publisher also got into trouble for printing a book titled Harry Potter in Calcutta.

(938) A blatant Russian rip-off of Harry Potter was the Tanya Grotter series of books by Dmitri Yemets. These books are not published in English because of legal action by JK Rowling but they were popular in Russia (which remains a law unto itself when it comes to copyright).

(939) In June 2005, Aaron Lambert, a security guard at a book distribution centre in Northamptonshire, stole a number of pages from Harry Potter and the Half-Blood Prince six weeks before its intended publication date. He was arrested a day later after negotiations to sell them to a journalist.

(940) Stuart Craig, the production designer on the films, said that JK Rowling gave him a map of Hogwarts and the lake, forest and station so that he could get the geography right.

(941) Piccadilly Circus features in Harry Potter and the Deathly Hallows Part 1. Piccadilly Circus is a bustling area in London's West End.

(942) Hogwarts may be inspired by Olympus in Greek Mythology. Mount Olympus is the highest mountain in Greece. Due to its majesty, remoteness, and beauty, it was only natural for the Ancient Greeks to believe that it is also the home of their most important gods since very early times.

(943) In 2006, a genus of pachycephalosaur dinosaur was discovered. Because it had a dragon like head it was named Dracorex hogswartsia - which means dragon king of Hogwarts.

(944) Harry Potter screenwriter Steve Kloves says he didn't like the scene in the film of Chamber of Secrets where Hagrid enters Hogwarts and the students applaud him. Kloves says Chris Columbus was responsible for this moment.

(945) Emma Watson's net worth is reportedly about $80 million.

(946) Papers and archives left by the late Alan Rickman suggest that he was frustrated at times by director David Yates. Rickman seemed to feel that Yates was disinterested in fully exploring Snape as a character.

(947) Snargaluff is a flesh-eating tree.

(948) If you want to make your own Butterbeer at home your best bet is to mix cream soda and butterscotch syrup and then put some cream on the top for the froth.

(949) Emma Watson said she cried when Sirius died in the film series.

(950) Evana Lynch says her favourite prop from the films was the lion head her character wore.

(951) Luna is the Latin name for the Greek Moon goddess Selene.

(952) In the Half-Blood Prince film, the location where Harry and Mr Weasley enter the phone box to descend into the Ministry of Magic is the junction of Scotland Place and Great Scotland Yard in London.

(953) Hagrid was a Gryffindor.

(954) Matthew Lewis said he was disappointed that the scene where Neville visits his parents in St Mungo's was not in the Order of the Phoenix film adaptation.

(955) Ollivanders Wand Shop in the films required 17,000 prop boxes all individually decorated.

(956) JK Rowling says she is happy for Harry Potter fan fiction to exist as long as the material is child friendly.

(957) One in every fifteen people in the world owns a Harry Potter book.

(958) The Wizarding World of Harry Potter theme park opened in Universal's Islands of Adventure in Florida in 2010. Attendance at the park jumped by 80% when this new attraction opened.

(959) When the first Harry Potter film was due for release, Warner Brothers began to take action against fan websites which used the name Harry Potter so that they could have exclusive control over this domain name. Their actions were criticised for being heavy-handed and mean-spirited,

especially as the people who set up these websites were the fans who made Harry Potter the phenomenon it was!

(960) Harry Potter merchandise in Britain has included Quidditch slippers, a Harry Potter egg cup, wand-shaped makeup brushes, and Hedwig lip balms.

(961) In a 2011 MTV poll, Chamber of Secrets was voted the worst film in the series.

(962) The Wizarding World of Harry Potter sold over one million mugs of Butterbeer during the 2010 winter holidays.

(963) Emma Watson says she was desperate to get the part of Hermione in the end. "I loved the books—I was a massive fan. I just felt like that part belonged to me. I know that sounds crazy, but from that first audition, I always knew. At the beginning, they were casting the other characters as well—but I always knew I was going out for Hermione. She came so naturally to me. Maybe so much of myself at the time was similar to her. Of course, all this terrified my parents—there were literally thousands and thousands of girls going out for the audition, and my parents were anxious about what I would do if I didn't get it."

(964) The Guardian's Peter Bradshaw gave the Half-Blood Prince film a very sniffy review. 'This latest Potter has some spectacular imagery, and director David Yates is a safe pair of hands; there are some nice moments and the tragic ending lands with a crash of timpani. But I feel an inexorable disenchantment with this franchise settling in, a sense of familiarity and stamina-loss amounting to a crisis of Potterist faith. Once, I believed that the films could theoretically convert newcomers to fanhood, but they are actually for signed-up fans only: competently managed big-screen renderings of a lucrative brand. As drama, they are becoming more and more inert, crammed with tiny events and minor

characters that are spurious, pointless and, frankly, dull.'

(965) The Shell Cottage scenes in Harry Potter and the Deathly Hallows Part 1 were filmed in Pembrokeshire.

(966) The motorbike tunnel sequence in Harry Potter and the Deathly Hallows Part 1 was shot in Queensway Tunnel, Liverpool.

(967) JK Rowling says that Harry and Ron were the first two characters she created when she started working on the first book.

(968) Harry Potter and the Cursed Child is the most expensive nonmusical Broadway play in history, costing $68.5 million. Much of this money was spent though renovating the Lyric Theatre.

(969) When Emma Watson's contract came up for renewal in 2006 they persuaded her to stay by altering her schedule so that she could sit her school exams. "It was mainly to do with scheduling and I had a real fight on my hands to ensure that I was able to go to university and I was able to sit my A-levels, because the schedule they handed to me didn't really allow for any of that and I just wasn't prepared to let it go. They essentially moved the Harry Potter film schedule around my exam dates, which was amazing. It all worked out."

(970) JK Rowling was recognised with the Order of the Forest for demanding that publishers around the world print her books using eco-friendly paper.

(971) When asked during production on the last film if she hung out with Daniel Radcliffe and Rupert Grint in real-life, Emma Watson said - "To be honest, we see so much of each other when we're working that hanging out together would be overload. I love them, but I need to see other friends off set.

They're like my siblings now. We're three different people, too. We will always be very important to each other. But, at the same time, after eight Harry Potter films, we'll be ready to go and do other things, and be other people, and have time for ourselves."

(972) When Alan Rickman died, Daniel Radcliffe said - "Alan Rickman is undoubtedly one of the greatest actors I will ever work with. He is also, one of the loyalest and most supportive people I've ever met in the film industry. He was so encouraging of me both on set and in the years post-Potter. I'm pretty sure he came and saw everything I ever did on stage both in London and New York. He didn't have to do that. I know other people who've been friends with him for much much longer than I have and they all say if you call Alan, it doesn't matter where in the world he is or how busy he is with what he's doing, he'll get back to you within a day."

(973) JK Rowling says she regrets pairing up Ron and Hermione and thinks Harry and Hermione should have ended up together.

(974) Pomona was a minor Roman goddess of fruit trees.

(975) Alan Rickman swiped a stash of Gringotts coins from the Harry Potter set.

(976) Jason Isaacs said that he tried to steal a copy of The Daily Prophet from the set to take home but was told to give it back!

(977) Black Park in Buckinghamshire doubled for the Dark Forest in the first film. Black Park covers over 500 acres of woodland, heathland and open space in South Buckinghamshire.

(978) In her Harvard speech, JK Rowling said - "I was convinced that the only thing I wanted to do, ever, was to

write novels. However, my parents, both of whom came from impoverished backgrounds and neither of whom had been to college, took the view that my overactive imagination was an amusing personal quirk that would never pay a mortgage, or secure a pension. I know that the irony strikes with the force of a cartoon anvil, now."

(979) The LA Times seemed thought that Goblet of Fire was the film that got the movie franchise into gear. 'It's taken them long enough, but the movies have finally gotten Harry Potter right. Despite the reported $2.7 billion earned by the series' three previous attempts, it's not until Harry Potter and the Goblet of Fire that a film has successfully re-created the sense of stirring magical adventure and engaged, edge-of-your-seat excitement that has made the books such an international phenomenon.'

(980) JK Rowling's advance for the first Harry Potter book was around £2,500 - a miniscule amount of money given how much they went on to generate.

(981) In the books, Hagrid is over 11 feet tall.

(982) The Dementors were inspired by JK Rowling's childhood nightmares.

(983) JK Rowling says that Goblet of Fire was the most difficult book to write because she had to go back and correct a big plot hole.

(984) TGI survey data found that Harry Potter was a more popular character for young people than Batman, Superman, or Spider-Man.

(985) In a 2011 MTV poll, Bellatrix Lestrange was voted the best villain with 31% of the vote.

(986) Daniel Radcliffe is estimated to have a net worth of around $110 million. This makes him the wealthiest Harry Potter cast member.

(987) Robert Pattinson is the second wealthiest Harry Potter cast member with a net worth of $100 million.

(988) JK Rowling considered giving Neville the last names Sidebottom or Pupp.

(989) Harry Potter And The Philosopher's Stone is called Harrius Potter et Philosophi Lapis in Latin.

(990) The name Narcissa is the female version of Narcissus. In Greek Mythology, Narcissus was a man who saw himself in the water and fell in love with his reflection.

(991) Orlando's Wizarding World of Harry Potter sells Butterbeer Fudge and Butterbeer Clotted Cream.

(992) Aunt Marge Dursley was based on JK Rowling's grandmother Frieda - a woman who Rowling says liked her dogs more than she did her human relatives.

(993) In a 2011 MTV poll, there was a tie between McGonagall and Lupin when it came to who fans thought was their favorite teacher.

(994) 200 mythical creatures have been created for the Harry Potter film series.

(995) Daniel Radcliffe says that his favourite Harry Potter films are Order of the Phoenix and Deathly Hallows Part 2. "I love the last one, but I also really love the fifth, which is not a lot of people's favourite, I kind of realise. I love it because of the relationship between Harry and Sirius [Black], and you get a lot of Gary Oldman in that movie. That was my favourite

one. Probably to film as well. We had a really, really good time making that one."

(996) In a 2019, ComingSoon.Net poll, fans were overwhelmingly against the idea of rebooting or remaking the Harry Potter films one day. They did say though that they wouldn't mind a new series of films featuring Harry's son.

(997) A Film Junk poll in 2011 voted Harry Potter and the Prisoner of Azkaban the best of the films with 48.3% of the vote.

(998) Tonks' patronus used to be a jackrabbit, but it changed to a wolf when she fell in love with Lupin.

(999) Grimmauld Place is obviously a riff on 'Grim Old Place'.

(1000) People from around the world can actually compete in international Quidditch tournaments. Sadly, there are no flying broomsticks though.

Lightning Source UK Ltd.
Milton Keynes UK
UKHW021046060722
405457UK00008B/1593